QUICK AND EASY STIR-FRIES AND OTHER DISHES FROM THE FAR EAST

Oriental Express

RECIPES COMPILED BY MAGGIE HARRADINE

QUICK AND EASY STIR-FRIES AND OTHER DISHES FROM THE FAR EAST

Oriental Express

RECIPES COMPILED BY MAGGIE HARRADINE

LIFESTYLE

和
愛
寿

Original recipes by Charlotte Coleman-Smith, Fiona Smith,
Dan Askham and Joanna Lamiri

Publisher: Lisa Simpson
Designer: Emily Cook
Picture researcher: Sarah Epton

This edition first published in Great Britain in 2000 by
LifeStyle
An imprint of Parkgate Books
London House, Great Eastern Wharf, Parkgate Road,
London SW11 4NQ

© Parkgate Books
A Division of Collins and Brown

A CIP catalogue record for this book is available from
the British Library.

ISBN 1-902617-19-3

PRINTED AND BOUND IN CHINA

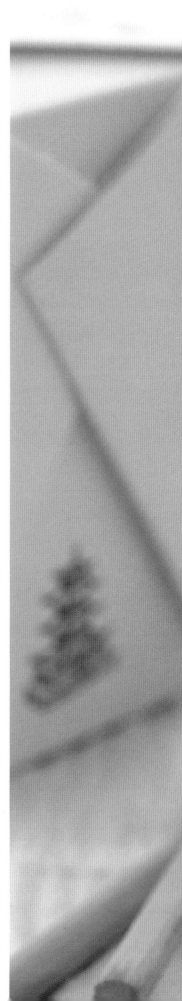

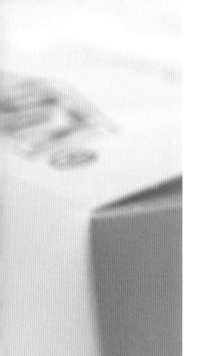

Introduction

The special combination of herbs and spices used in preparing oriental dishes are what give the foods of China, Thailand, Vietnam and Malaysia their distinctive character and flavour, both within the Far East and throughout the world. However, the recipes and flavours change not only from country to country but also regionally with striking differences in the North, South and Central areas. For instance, in China there are essentially four schools of cuisine, each with their own particular specialities and taste; Peking, Shanghai, Szechuan and Canton.

In the West, the majority of "Chinese" restaurants actually serve the Cantonese style of food. These dishes, by tradition, tend to be lightly cooked due to the historical lack of fuel for cooking. But to the Western pallette, the subtlety of flavours associated with this style of cooking – which is dominated by stir-frying – has meant an ever increasing growth in the popularity of oriental food.

So, when we think of oriental food, we think predominantly of stir-frying which is a technique whereby small pieces of food are quickly fried over a high heat until just tender. To create the perfect stir-fry, food is cut into similar size pieces which are then added to a wok or frying pan in stages, depending on how long the ingredient will take to cook. Meat and poultry are generally the first to go into the wok with vegetables being added later so as to retain a slight crunch. When you have little time available, stir-frying is a great method as cooking times are normally brief and it is possible to cook an entire meal in one pan. It should also be noted that stir-frying is a very healthy way of cooking as only a small amount of oil or fat is needed and quick cooking ensures that the food does not become saturated in fat. It is essential that the oil is really hot before you add the ingredients and that when added to the wok or pan, the ingredients are stirred constantly and vigorously during cooking.

From the delicately flavoured and aromatic to the hot and spicy, there is something in oriental cooking to suit every taste, and you will soon find yourself adapting recipes and developing your own variations.

There are certain ingredients and equipment that you will come across whilst trying the recipes in this book, so before you begin to cook, take time to read this section which provides a basic guide:

WOK – In addition to being essential for stir fries, this bowl shaped pan is also an incredibly versatile piece of equipment when cooking oriental food, as it is used in the cooking of soups, rice dishes and noodle dishes. It is worthwhile therefore investing in a good quality wok, and ensuring that you follow the purchase instructions for seasoning the wok and keeping it clean. Woks are now available in many different metals – the most traditional of which is cast iron – but beware of stainless steel as these have a tendency to scorch and "non-stick" woks end up invariably being more expensive and not necessarily living up to their name.

BAMBOO STEAMER – These are relatively inexpensive and should rest snugly inside the wok on it's slopping sides (without touching the surface of the water) for steaming vegetables and pancakes.

CHOPSTICKS – As well as being the oriental equivalent to our knife and fork, the chopstick is a useful tool to have around the kitchen as they are great for fluffing up rice and seperating noodles during cooking.

BAMBOO SHOOTS – widely available either in tins or fresh, these are the soft shoots of the bamboo plant.

BEAN SPROUTS – from the mung bean, these add texture to stir-fries but have very little flavour.

CHINESE 5 SPICE POWDER – traditional aromatic flavouring containing anise, pepper, fennel, clovers and cinnamon.

CREAMED COCONUT – not to be mistaken with coconut milk, this is a thick paste with an intense coconut flavour.

FISH SAUCE – with a pungent aroma, but delicate taste this sauce is made from the liquid which drains off salted packed fish.

GALANGAL – a member of the ginger family, which tastes like a cross between pepper and mild ginger.

GINGER – the fresh root has a warm, sweetish aroma, but its flavour is hot and slightly biting. To prepare fresh ginger, peel off the brown skin. Grate or cut the required amount. Alternatively, crush with the flat side of a knife to loosen the fibres, then chop finely.

HOISIN (Hoi Sin) SAUCE – a thick, sweet tasting sauce made from fermented soy beans, red rice, salt and sugar.

KAFFIR LIME LEAVES – fragrant lime flavoured leaves, usually crushed or shredded. Leaves can be bought fresh or dried.

LEMON GRASS – this herb imparts a mild, sour-sweet cirtus flavour. To prepare fresh lemon grass, peel away the outer layer and use the tender root end, finely chopped.

OYSTER SAUCE – made from oyster and seafood extract, this is used in many fish dishes.

PAK CHOI – this is Chinese mustard cabbage with a crisp texture, sweet and mild in flavour.

PANCAKES – these are savoury, wafer thin and made from flour and water.

PLUM SAUCE – this is a sweet and sour sauce with a unique fruity flavour, typically served with duck.

RICE WINE (Shao Hsing) – this has a sweet sherry-like flavour, and in fact sherry can be used as a substitute.

SHALLOTS – mild flavoured member of the onion family.

SHIITAKE MUSHROOMS – these mushrooms have a very distinctive texture and meaty flavour.

SOY SAUCE – the stable of many recipes, made from naturally fermented soy beans.

SPRING ROLL WRAPPERS – made from wheat, these are easy to use provided you follow the packet instructions.

SZECHUAN PEPPERCORNS – not as strong as white or black peppercorns, they add a unique aromatic taste.

TAHINI – this is a paste made from toasted sesame seeds and is used, as is sesame seed oil, predominantly for its strong flavour.

TOFU (To Fu) – also known as bean curd, readily absorbs the flavours of the food it is cooked with.

WATER CHESTNUTS – these are available tinned at supermarkets and are crunchy with a mild flavour. Serve sliced into disks.

YELLOW BEAN SAUCE – a thick paste made from salted, fermented yellow soy beans, crushed with flour and sugar.

Lemon grass soup

Serves 4

METHOD

Cut the chicken across the grain into thin equal sized strips. Pour the stock into the saucepan with the lemon grass, lime juice, fish sauce, lime zest, chillies and sugar. Simmer for 5 minutes. Add the chicken strips and cook at just below simmering point for 2-3 minutes until they are cooked.

Serve the soup in hot bowls garnished with coriander leaves.

INGREDIENTS

175-225g/6-8oz chicken breast
600ml/1 pint chicken stock
2 fat stalks lemon grass, finely chopped
3 tbsp lime juice
1 tbsp fish sauce
1¼ tbsp grated lime zest
½ fresh red chilli, thinly sliced
½ fresh green chilli, thinly sliced
pinch of sugar
coriander leaves, to garnish

Easy peking-style chicken

Serves 2

METHOD

This is not a traditional recipe, but it makes it easy to recreate Peking flavours. Mix together the marinade ingredients in a large non-metal bowl and cover the chicken. Marinade the chicken for at least 2 hours, preferably overnight.

Preheat the oven to 180°C/350°F/Gas Mark 4. Place the chicken in a small roasting dish and pour over the marinade. Cook for about 20 minutes. Cool for about 5 minutes and slice. Have the warmed pancakes or rice ready with the other garnishes. Guests can make up their own pancakes or you can serve the chicken slices over the rice.

Julienned means to cut into thin equal sized batons or ribbons.

INGREDIENTS

2 chicken breasts, skinned

THE MARINADE

2 garlic cloves, crushed
1 tsp five spice powder
60ml/4 tbsp soy sauce
15ml/1 tbsp honey
10ml/2 tsp sesame oil
15ml/1 tbsp chilli sauce (optional)
Chinese style pancakes or boiled rice
½ cucumber, julienned
6 spring onions, shredded
plum or hoisin sauce

Thai-style seafood salad

Serves 4

METHOD

Drain the seafood, reserving the oil. Slice the pepper and finely chop the red chilli. Grate the rind of the limes, then halve them and squeeze the juice into a small bowl.

Heat the oil, reserved from the jars of seafood, then add the garlic, lime leaves, sliced pepper, chilli, lemon grass, lime juice and lime rind and cook for about 2-3 minutes. Remove from the heat and pour over the seafood. Season generously with salt and ground black pepper. Leave in a cool place to marinate for about 1 hour. Serve on a bed of salad leaves and garnish with lemon wedges.

INGREDIENTS

2 x 290g/10oz jars prepared seafood in oil
½ red pepper, sliced
1 small red chilli, finely chopped
2 limes
1 garlic clove, crushed
3 kaffir lime leaves
1 stalk lemon grass
salt and ground black pepper
salad leaves to serve
lemon wedges to garnish (optional)

Ensure that you wash your hands thoroughly after handling chillies.

Sweet and sour pork with pineapple

Serves 4

METHOD

Season the pork with salt and pepper and lightly coat it with flour. Sauté the onion, garlic, ginger and peppers for 3–4 minutes in the butter and oil. Remove the mixture from the pan.

Add the meat to the pan and seal on all sides for 2–3 minutes. Return the onion mixture to the pan and stir in 55g (2oz) flour. Add the stock and tomato purée and stir well. Add all the remaining ingredients and cook until tender. Adjust the seasoning to taste and serve with rice and green salad.

INGREDIENTS

685g/1lb 8oz diced pork
1 large onion, diced
1 red pepper, diced
1 yellow pepper, diced
1 tin of pineapple chunks
55g/2oz flour
30g/1oz butter
425ml/¾ pint chicken stock
55g/2oz sugar
½ tbsp tomato purée
½ tbsp light soy sauce
30g/1oz root ginger
1 garlic clove, crushed
60ml/2fl oz white wine vinegar or distilled
malt vinegar
plain flour for coating pork
vegetable oil
salt and pepper

Vietnamese grilled fish

Serves 2

METHOD

Remove the scales from the fish, rinse and pat dry with paper towels. Make three diagonal slashes across both sides of the fish, rub the salt into the skin and brush 1 tbsp of the lime juice all over the fish. Place the fish in a glass dish and set aside for 15 minutes.

Shred the Kaffir leaves and place them in the cavity of each fish. Put the ingredients for the baste into a food processor with the remaining lime juice and blend to a paste. Spread the baste all over the fish and set them aside for another 20 minutes.

Grill the fish in a wire basket or wrapped in a double thickness of foil for 15-20 minutes under a hot grill, turning once. Alternatively, cook on a lightly oiled griddle pan.

If you are unsure, ask for your fish to be cleaned and gutted at the fishmonger.

INGREDIENTS

675g/1½ lb fish such as small salmon, bass, bream or snapper, gutted
½ tsp salt
3 tbsp lime juice
2 Kaffir leaves

FOR THE BASTE

1 tbsp light soy sauce
1 tbsp fish sauce
5cm/2inch piece fresh ginger root, roughly chopped
1 shallot, peeled
1 red chilli, seeded and chopped
1 bulb lemon grass, roughly chopped
1 garlic clove, chopped
½ tsp ground galangal

Chicken strips with sesame seeds

Serves 2

METHOD

You can serve this deliciously tangy dish with noodles, rice or pasta – or on top of a green salad of mixed leaves.

Heat the oil in a wok and stir-fry the sesame seeds with the spring onions for 1 minute. Add the chicken and stir-fry for another 5 minutes. Stir in the soy sauce and the chilli sauce, then add the coriander, if using, and the sesame oil. Season to taste and serve.

You could always try this dish with pork or turkey rather than chicken. Also, try adding a pinch of grated ginger for extra spice.

INGREDIENTS

1 tbsp sunflower oil
1-2 tbsp sesame seeds
2 spring onions, chopped
2 skinned chicken breasts, cut into strips
or chunks
1 tbsp soy sauce
few drops of chilli sauce or one or two
fresh chillies, chopped
coriander leaves, roughly chopped
(optional)
1 tsp sesame oil
rice, noodles, or pasta

Oriental salmon steaks

Serves 4

METHOD

Brush each salmon steak generously with the teriyaki sauce. Peel and slice the ginger and spring onions. Place a few slices of ginger and the chopped spring onions on top of each of the salmon steaks.

Leave the steaks in a cool place for at least 30 minutes to marinate. Grill the steaks under a medium grill for about 5 minutes on each side or until cooked through

When the fish is opaque, remove from the grill and serve immediately on a bed of egg noodles (readily available from the supermarket).

INGREDIENTS

4 salmon steaks
teriyaki marinade sauce for brushing
small piece of root ginger, peeled and sliced
2 spring onions, finely chopped
noodles to serve

Spicy fried rice

Serves 4

METHOD

Cook the jasmine rice according to the packet instructions. Next place the beans in a saucepan of boiling water and boil for 2 minutes. Drain and refresh under cold water, then drain again.

Heat the oil in a wok, add the onion, garlic and chillies and cook until the onion has softened. Stir in the nam prik and continue to cook for 3-4 minutes. Add the chicken and stir-fry for 2 minutes. Stir in the rice until it is well coated, then push to the sides of the wok. Pour the eggs into the centre of the wok.

When just beginning to set, mix evenly into the rice, adding the fish sauce at the same time. Stir in the prawns then transfer to a shallow, warmed serving dish and garnish with chilli, coriander and spring onions.

INGREDIENTS

175g/6oz Thai jasmine rice
115g/4oz French green beans, cut into
2.5cm/1inch lengths
2 tbsp vegetable oil
1 large onion, finely chopped
3 garlic cloves, chopped
1 fresh green chilli, finely chopped
2 tbsp Nam Prik
85g/3oz chicken, diced
2 eggs, beaten
1 tbsp fish sauce
55g/2oz cooked shelled prawns or shrimp
finely sliced red chilli, shredded coriander
leaves and diagonally sliced spring onions
for garnish

Chinese stir-fry

Serves 4

METHOD

Vary the ingredients in this dish according to the vegetables you have available – use this recipe as a guide.

Cook the noodles according to the packet instructions. Drain, toss with the soy sauce to taste, then set aside. Heat the oil in a wok, add the mangetouts, carrots, pepper, sweet corn, garlic and ginger and stir-fry for 2 minutes.

Add the beansprouts, chilli sauce and stock and stir-fry for another 2-3 minutes. Serve with the noodles. Sprinkle with a little sesame oil and snip some fresh herbs or spring onions over the top.

INGREDIENTS

170g/6oz dried egg noodles
1 tbsp soy sauce
1 tbsp sunflower oil
110g/4oz mangetouts, trimmed
55g/2oz carrots, sliced diagonally
half a red pepper, sliced
55g/2oz baby sweetcorn, left whole
1 garlic clove, crushed
½ tbsp grated fresh ginger
55g/2oz beansprouts
few drops of chilli sauce
2 tbsp vegetable stock or water

Balinese duck

Serves 4

METHOD

Mix the paste ingredients together until smooth. Remove the fat from the duck, then prick it with a skewer. Using a sharp knife, cut slashes in the breast and put 2 spoonfuls of paste in the cavity of the duck.

Spread the paste evenly over the duck, ensuring it goes into the slashes then place on a rack in a baking dish. Cover loosely with foil and leave for 2 hours, or refrigerate overnight. Preheat oven to 180°C/350°F/Gas Mark 4. Remove the foil and roast for about 2¼ hours, basting frequently. Transfer the duck to a warmed plate. Pour the cooking juices into a pan.

Remove the duck flesh from the bones and pile on to a warmed plate. Cover and keep warm. Remove the fat from the cooking juices and boil the juices hard until reduced and thickened. Pour over the duck and scatter coriander leaves.

INGREDIENTS

2-2.25kg/4½-5lb duck
leaves from a bunch of coriander

FOR THE PASTE

2 garlic cloves
3 fresh green chillies
1 tbsp roasted coriander seeds
3 fresh bay leaves
2 tbsp soy sauce
2 tbsp oyster sauce
2 tbsp lime juice
1 tbsp peanut oil
2 tbsp light brown sugar
5cm/2inch fresh ginger root

Chicken noodle soup

Serves 4

METHOD

This traditional dish is very simple to make and a great way to use up any left over roast chicken.

Put the stock in a saucepan and bring to the boil. Sprinkle in the vermicelli and stir, to ensure it does not stick together, until the stock returns to the boil again.

Add the spring onions with the seasoning and cook for 6-8 minutes until the pasta is cooked. Add the chopped chicken and parsley and heat through to serve.

INGREDIENTS

900ml/1½ pints chicken stock
50g/2oz vermicelli, broken up
4 spring onions, sliced
salt and pepper to taste
50g/2oz cooked chicken, chopped
1 tbsp chopped parsley

Indonesian crab cakes

Serves 2

METHOD

Cook the rice according to the packet instructions. Put the spring onion, lemon grass, cashew nuts, chilli, ginger and coriander in a food processor and blend until everything is finely chopped.

Add the rice, crab meat, soy sauce and egg and blend a little longer until all the ingredients are combined. Do not allow the mixture to become a purée. Chill for 1 hour.

Mould the mixture into 8 small patties and brush them with oil. Place on a hot, oiled griddle plate under the grill for about 8-10 minutes, turning frequently until golden brown. Serve hot with thinly shredded vegetables.

INGREDIENTS

Serves 4 as a starter
55g/2oz long-grain rice
3 spring onions, chopped
5cm/2inch piece lemon grass, chopped
10 cashew nuts
½ red chilli
1 tsp grated fresh ginger root
1 tbsp chopped fresh coriander
225g/8oz tinned white crab meat, drained
2 tsp light soy sauce
1 small egg, beaten
oil

Cabbage, potato and rice soup

Serves 2

METHOD

This is a simple, filling and delicious soup with a hint of the orient. If you prefer your food spicy, add a dash of either soy sauce or Tabasco to enhance the flavour.

Heat the oil in a large saucepan and sauté the garlic, onion, cumin and potato for about 5 minutes. Stir in the rice and cabbage and then add the stock.

Bring to the boil, then turn down to a simmer and cook for about 20 minutes. Season with salt and pepper and serve with crusty bread.

INGREDIENTS

15ml/1 tbsp olive oil
2 garlic cloves, finely sliced
1 onion, sliced
2 tsp whole cumin seeds
50g/½oz long grain rice
1 large potato, peeled and cubed
200g/6½oz cabbage, sliced
1 litre/1¾ pints of vegetable stock
salt and pepper

Spiced beef bites

Serves 4

METHOD

Put the steak into a bowl. Stir together
the chilli, garlic, ginger and cream. Pour
over the steak, stir, then cover and leave
in the refrigerator for 3 hours. Put the
breadcrumbs in a shallow dish.

Dip a few cubes of meat at a time into
the egg, allow the excess to drain off,
then roll in the breadcrumbs to coat
evenly.

Heat a 2.5cm (1inch) layer of oil in a
large frying pan over a medium heat.
Add the beef in batches so that the pan
is never crowded and fry, turning
occasionally, until golden and crisp on
the outside and cooked to taste inside.
Using a slotted spoon, transfer on to
paper towels to drain.

INGREDIENTS

700g/1½ lb sirloin steak, cut into
2.5cm/1inch cubes
2 green chillies, very finely chopped
1 garlic clove, crushed
2 tsp grated ginger
4 tbsp double cream
salt
85g/3oz dried breadcrumbs
1 large egg, beaten
vegetable oil, for frying

Serves 4

Glazed lamb

INGREDIENTS

450g/1lb boneless lean lamb
15ml/1 tbsp grapeseed oil
175g/6oz mangetouts, topped and tailed
3 spring onions, sliced
30ml/2 tbsp clear honey
Juice of ½ lemon
2 tbsp chopped fresh coriander
1 tbsp sesame seeds
salt and ground black pepper

METHOD

Using a sharp knife, cut the lamb into equal shaped thin strips. Heat the oil in the wok and then stir-fry the lamb until browned all over. Remove from the wok and keep warm. Now place the mangetouts and spring onions in the wok and stir-fry for about 30 seconds.

Put the lamb back into the wok and add the honey, lemon juice, chopped coriander and sesame seeds. Season well with salt and pepper, stirring thoroughly to coat the lamb and vegetables with the glaze. Bring the wok to the boil, then allow to bubble vigorously for about a minute. Remove from the pan and serve with rice or noodles.

Serves 4

Scented lemon noodles

INGREDIENTS

250g/8oz rice noodles
3 tbsp olive or groundnut oil
½ garlic clove, crushed
2.5cm/1inch piece fresh root ginger, grated
1 large red or green chilli, seeded and thinly sliced
2 stalks lemon grass
3 spring onions, sliced
50g/2oz salted peanuts, roughly chopped
salt and pepper to taste

If lemon grass is not obtainable, substitute with grated rind and juice of ½ a lemon and ½ tsp brown sugar. **ⓘ**

METHOD

Cook the rice noodles according to the packet instructions. Meanwhile, heat the oil in a wok. Add the garlic, ginger and chilli and stir-fry for 1 minute. Grate the bulb end of the lemon grass. Add to the wok with the spring onions and peanuts. Continue stir-frying for about 30 seconds.

Drain the cooked noodles and add to the wok. Heat through, tossing well together. Add the seasoning and serve immediately.

Hot and sour soup

METHOD

Squeeze the soaked mushrooms dry, then discard the hard stalks. Thinly shred the mushrooms, meat, tofu and bamboo shoots. Bring the stock to a fast boil in a wok and add the shredded ingredients. Bring back to the boil and simmer for about 1 minute. Add the wine or sherry, soy sauce and vinegar and season. Bring back to the boil, then add the cornflour paste, stir until thickened and serve.

INGREDIENTS

4-6 Chinese mushrooms, soaked in warm water
115g/4oz pork or chicken
1 packet tofu
50g/2oz sliced bamboo shoots, drained
600ml/1 pint stock
15ml/1 tbsp Chinese rice wine or dry sherry
15ml/1 tbsp light soy sauce
15ml/1 tbsp rice vinegar
salt and ground white pepper
1 tbsp cornflour paste

Thai spring rolls

METHOD

To make the filling, drain and chop the mushrooms and the noodles. Heat the oil in a wok, add the garlic and chillies and fry for 30 seconds. Add the pork (stirring until the meat is browned), noodles, mushrooms and prawns. Season with fish sauce, sugar and pepper then tip into a bowl. Add the carrot, bamboo shoots, beansprouts, spring onions and coriander.

Place a spoonful of filling in the centre of a spring roll wrapper. Turn the bottom edge over to cover the filling, then fold in the left and right sides. Roll the wrapper up almost to the top edge. Brush the top edge with flour paste and seal. Heat the oil in a wok and fry the spring rolls a few at a time until crisp and golden brown.

INGREDIENTS

4-6 dried Chinese mushrooms, soaked
50g/2oz bean thread noodles, soaked
30ml/2 tbsp vegetable oil
2 garlic cloves, chopped
2 red chillies, seeded and chopped
225g/8oz minced pork
50g/2oz chopped cooked prawns
30ml/2 tbsp fish sauce
1 tsp granulated sugar
1 carrot, finely shredded
50g/2oz bamboo shoots, chopped
50g/2oz beansprouts
2 spring onions, chopped
1 tbsp chopped coriander
24x15cm/6inch square spring roll wrappers
freshly ground black pepper
oil for frying
Thai sweet chilli sauce, for dipping

FOR THE FLOUR PASTE

2 tbsp flour
water

Stir-fried spinach

METHOD

Remove the stalks from the spinach and tear the leaves into large pieces. Add to a large saucepan of boiling water and blanch for 45 seconds. Drain the spinach and rinse immediately under cold running water, then squeeze hard in a colander until completely dry.

Heat a wok over a high heat until very hot, add the oil and heat. Add the garlic, chillies and ginger. Toss for a few seconds, then add the spinach rapidly, tossing quickly to separate pieces and coat with oil. Sprinkle with a little oyster sauce, toss and serve immediately.

INGREDIENTS

450g/1 lb fresh spinach
1 tbsp peanut oil
1 garlic clove, finely crushed
1 fresh green chilli, chopped
1 fresh red chilli, chopped
1 tsp finely chopped ginger root
oyster sauce

和愛寿

Serves 4-6

METHOD

Cut the chicken breasts into long strips about 5mm (¼inch) thick and 1.25cm (½inch) wide. Place them in a glass dish. Mix the ingredients for the marinade, stirring until the sugar dissolves. Pour over the chicken and leave to marinate for 1 hour.

Thread the chicken on to the skewers and cook on a lightly oiled griddle plate over a prepared barbecue for 5-6 minutes, turning them over halfway and brushing them with the marinade. Serve garnished with spring onion tassels and cucumber fans.

> Soak some long bamboo skewers in water for 30 minutes before use to prevent burning.

Chicken teriyaki

INGREDIENTS

4 large boneless, skinless chicken breasts
½ cucumber, for garnish
spring onion tassels, for garnish

FOR THE TERIYAKI MARINADE

2 tbsp oil
2 tbsp soy sauce
1 tbsp brown ginger
2 tbsp rice wine or dry sherry
1 tsp grated fresh ginger root
1 garlic clove, crushed

Fast sweet and sour stir-fry

Serves 4-6

METHOD

Heat the oil in a wok until very hot. The secret of a good stir-fry is to ensure that the temperature of the oil is hot enough, and that the food is moved quickly around the wok, not absorbing the oil.

Add the peppers and onions to the wok and stir-fry for about 4 minutes. In a separate bowl, mix together the pineapple juice, tomato purée, soy sauce, vinegar and cornflour.

Add to the vegetables and bring to the boil. Simmer for 2 minutes. Add the remaining ingredients and stir-fry for another 2 minutes. Serve with rice or noodles.

> You can test to see whether the oil is hot enough by adding a small piece of pepper to the pan and checking that it 'sizzles'.

INGREDIENTS

2 tbsp sunflower oil
1 red or yellow pepper, deseeded and diced
1 green pepper, deseeded and diced
small bunch spring onions, chopped
200g/7oz tinned pineapple chunks,
plus 3 tbsp juice
1 tbsp tomato purée
2 tbsp soy sauce
1 tbsp white wine vinegar
2 tsp cornflour
handful of cashew nuts, peanuts or pine nuts
200g/7oz beansprouts
rice or noodles

Squid salad with lime dressing

27

Serves 2

METHOD

Heat a large frying pan or wok to very hot and add 15ml (1 tbsp) of the oil. Whilst the pan and oil are heating, cut the squid. If the squid is small, slice down one side, to open out and criss-cross slash one side. If the squid is large, slice into 2cm (1inch) wide rings.

Now add the squid and the next 4 ingredients to the pan and quickly stir-fry until the squid is cooked, which should take about 2 minutes. Take the pan off the heat, remove the squid and add the fish sauce, lime juice and remaining oil to the pan. Do not put the pan back on the heat as the contents of the pan will burn, so allow to warm thoroughly using the heat of the pan. Divide the salad and avocado between 2 plates, top with squid and drizzle with dressing. Scatter with fresh coriander.

INGREDIENTS

400g/14oz cleaned squid bodies and tentacles (optional)
30ml/2 tbsp groundnut oil
3cm/1½inch fresh ginger, grated
1–2 mild red chillies, deseeded and finely chopped
1 garlic clove, crushed
2 sticks of lemon grass, peeled and finely sliced
30ml/2 tbsp Thai fish sauce
15ml/1 tbsp lime juice
150g/5oz mixed salad leaves
1 small avocado, chopped
15g/½oz fresh coriander, chopped

Chinese chicken stir-fry

Serves 2

METHOD

Place the chicken strips in a dish. Mix the cornflour with the soy sauce in a cup, then pour it over the chicken and leave to marinate for 30 minutes to 1 hour if possible (the longer the better).

Heat the oil in a wok, add the chicken and cook briefly on all sides, then transfer to a plate. Add the onion, garlic, ginger, broccoli, mushrooms and spring onions and stir-fry for 2 minutes. Add a little salt to taste, then return the chicken to the pan, add the sherry, cover with a lid and cook for a further 3-4 minutes. Meanwhile, cook the noodles according to the packet instructions. Drain and toss with the soy sauce to taste. Serve the chicken on the bed of noodles.

INGREDIENTS

2 skinned chicken breasts, cut into strips
1 tbsp cornflour
140ml/5fl oz soy sauce, plus 1 tbsp for
tossing with noodles
1 tbsp sunflower oil
½ onion, finely chopped
1 garlic clove, finely chopped
½ tbsp grated fresh ginger
85g/3oz broccoli, sliced
85g/3oz mushrooms, sliced
2 spring onions, finely chopped
salt
1 tbsp sherry
egg noodles

Thai vegetable curry

Serves 4

METHOD

Heat the oil in a large pan or wok, then add the onion, garlic and carrots. Cook for about 10 minutes until soft, then add the potatoes, curry paste, coconut milk, stock, lemon grass and lime leaves.

Bring to the boil then simmer for about 20 minutes. Stir in the pepper, mangetout and baby corn and cook for a further 5-10 minutes until heated through but still retaining some crunch. Meanwhile, in a large pan of boiling, salted water, cook the noodles or rice.

Once all the vegetables are cooked, but still crunchy, remove from the pan and serve with either noodles or rice. You could use Thai rice, available from major supermarkets.

Try adding chicken or king prawns to this recipe, but ensure they are thoroughly cooked.

INGREDIENTS

1 tbsp oil
1 large onion, chopped
1 garlic clove, crushed
170g/6oz carrots, sliced on the diagonal
170g/6oz small new potatoes
4 tbsp green curry paste
300ml/½ pint coconut milk
300ml/½ vegetable stock
1 stalk lemon grass
3 kaffir lime leaves
1 large red pepper, thinly sliced
110g/4oz mangetout
110g/4oz baby corn on the cob
noodles or rice to serve

Stir-fried prawns and beansprouts with peanut sauce

Serves 4-6

METHOD

Place the noodles in a pan of boiling, salted water. Remove the pan from the heat immediately and leave to stand for 4–5 minutes, then drain. Meanwhile, chop the spring onions diagonally.

Heat the wok, add the oil and when smoking add the spring onions and garlic. Stir vigorously to prevent sticking for 1–2 minutes. Add the prawns and beansprouts and cook for 2–3 minutes more. Add the peanut butter, coconut milk and lemon juice. Stir well to make a smooth sauce. Heat through. Adjust the seasoning as necessary. Serve on a bed of noodles.

INGREDIENTS

2 x 250g/9oz packets thread egg noodles
450g/1lb frozen prawns or shrimp, defrosted
1 bunch spring onions
340g/12oz beansprouts
2 tbsp crunchy peanut butter
3 tbsp coconut milk
1 garlic clove, crushed
2 tbsp vegetable oil
salt and pepper
juice of 1 lemon

Aromatic duck with orange and ginger

Serves 4

METHOD

Using a sharp knife, make cuts in the duck skin in a diamond-like pattern. Brush with the honey and place the duck breasts in a glass dish. Mix the marinade ingredients together and pour over the duck. Cover and chill for at least 2 hours, or overnight.

Blend the cornflour into the marinade. Put the marinade in a pan with the stem ginger and orange juice and simmer until thickened. Remove the duck breasts and then brush with a little oil, place them under a hot grill, skin side up, and cook them for about 20 minutes, turning them once. Cut the duck into slices, arrange on warm serving plates, pour on a little sauce and garnish with orange slices or wedges.

INGREDIENTS

4 duck breasts, about 200g/7oz each
1 tbsp honey
1 tbsp oil
1 small orange, sliced or cut into wedges
for garnish

FOR THE AROMATIC MARINADE

2 tbsp dark soy sauce
1 tsp grated fresh ginger root
1 garlic clove, crushed
grated rind and juice of 1 large orange
pinch of five-spice powder
1 bulb lemon grass, finely chopped

FOR THE ORANGE GINGER SAUCE

2 tsp cornflour
2 tsp finely chopped stem ginger
250ml/8fl oz orange juice

Thai fried noodles

Serves 4

METHOD

Heat the oil in a wok or large frying pan, add the garlic and cook, stirring occasionally, until it starts to turn golden. Stir in the chillies and cook for 1-2 minutes. Stir in the fish sauce, lime juice and sugar until the sugar has dissolved. Stir in the eggs quickly and cook for a few seconds. Stir in the noodles until well coated, then add 85g (3oz) of the prawns and 85g (3oz) of the beansprouts, half the spring onions and coriander.

When the noodles are tender, transfer the contents of the wok or the pan to a serving dish and garnish with the remaining prawns, beansprouts and spring onions, peanuts, coriander leaves and lime slices.

INGREDIENTS

3 tbsp vegetable oil
4 garlic cloves, finely crushed
1 fresh red chilli, finely chopped
1 fresh green chilli, finely chopped
1 tbsp fish sauce
3-4 tbsp lime juice
1 tsp sugar
2 eggs, beaten
350g/12oz rice vermicelli, soaked in water for 20 minutes, drained
150g/5oz cooked shelled prawns or shrimp
115g/4oz beansprouts
4 spring onions, sliced
2 tbsp chopped coriander
finely chopped roasted peanuts, coriander leaves and lime slices, to garnish

和愛寿

Korean ribs

Serves 4

METHOD

Using a heavy sharp knife and mallet, cut the ribs into short lengths. Place them in a glass dish. Crush the sesame seeds lightly in a pestle and mortar, then mix them with the remaining marinade ingredients. Pour the marinade over the ribs and chill for at least 4 hours, but preferably overnight.

Lightly oil a grill rack and place the ribs on the rack under a hot grill to cook for about 15-20 minutes, turning them often and basting with the marinade during cooking.

INGREDIENTS

1.4kg/3lb pork ribs

FOR THE KOREAN MARINADE

1 tbsp toasted sesame seeds
2 garlic cloves, crushed
2 tsp grated fresh ginger root
2 tsp sesame oil
5 tbsp dark soy sauce
1 tbsp honey
1 small onion, very finely chopped
1 tsp chilli sauce (optional)

Stir-fried chicken with onions, coriander and lime

Serves 4-6

METHOD

Place the noodles in a pan of boiling, salted water. Remove the pan from the heat immediately and leave to stand for 4–5 minutes, then drain. Meanwhile, thinly slice the chicken and cut the spring onions diagonally.

Remove the coriander leaves from the stalks and squeeze the juice from the limes. Heat the oil in the wok until smoking. Add the chicken and stir vigorously. Cook for 2–3 minutes. Add the spring onions and fry for 2–3 minutes more. Add the lime juice, salt, pepper and coriander. Cook for 2 minutes more. Serve on a bed of noodles.

INGREDIENTS

2 x 250g/9oz packets thread egg noodles
685g/1lb 8oz chicken breast (skinless)
2 bunches spring onions
1 bunch fresh coriander
the juice of 3 limes
2 tbsp vegetable oil
salt and pepper

Stir-fried shredded beef

Serves 4-6

METHOD

Place the noodles in a pan of boiling, salted water. Remove the pan from the heat immediately and leave to stand for 4-5 minutes, then drain. Meanwhile, slice the beef into thin slices (the thinner the slices, the quicker they will cook).

Shred or thinly slice the mushrooms. Chop the chillies (the heat lies mostly in the pith and seeds so discard these if you don't like too much heat). Peel and chop the garlic and chop the onions diagonally. Heat the oil in the wok until smoking. Add the beef and stir-fry vigorously for 1-2 minutes. Add the onions and chilli. Cook for 2 minutes more, stirring constantly. Add the mushrooms and garlic and cook for a further 2-3 minutes. Add the soy sauce, stir, remove from the pan and serve on a bed of noodles.

INGREDIENTS

2 x 250g/9oz packets thread egg noodles
685g/1lb 8oz good-quality beef
450g/1lb mushrooms (oyster mushrooms work well)
4 green chillies
1 garlic clove
1 bunch spring onions
1 tbsp soy sauce
2 tbsp vegetable oil

Sweet and sour fish

Serves 2

METHOD

It is not always essential to stir fry food in oil. If the oil is not important for the flavour, food can be 'steam fried' in water, which will start the cooking process the same way.

Heat 100ml (3½fl oz) water in a medium pan. Place the onions, ginger, carrots, chilli and pepper in the pan and steam fry for about 2 minutes. Add the pineapple with juice, cornflour and vinegar and cook until thickened. Add the sugar (if needed) and a little salt. Grill or pan-fry the fish for about 5 minutes on each side and then pour over the sweet and sour sauce. Sweet and Sour sauce tastes particularly good when served with rice.

INGREDIENTS

4 spring onions, shredded
3cm/1½inch fresh ginger, shredded
1 red chilli, sliced (optional)
2 medium carrots, julienned
1 red and green pepper, julienned
250g/8oz tinned pineapple chunks
2 tsp cornflour, slackened with
15ml/1 tbsp water
15ml/1 tbsp white wine vinegar
1 tsp sugar (optional)
2 x 150–200g/5–6½oz fillets of fish
salt

Cornflour needs to be mixed or 'slackened' with a small amount of water (15ml/1 tbsp) before it is combined with other ingredients to prevent it from forming lumps.

Spiced mushrooms

Serves 4

METHOD

This delicately flavoured dish is ideal as a starter or side dish.

With your hands, break the mushrooms into large pieces. Heat the olive oil in a wok or frying pan, add the garlic, ginger and peppercorns. Cook for 1-2 minutes, then stir in the mushrooms. Cook for 4-5 minutes, stirring occasionally. Stir in the sesame seeds for about 30 seconds. Serve immediately.

INGREDIENTS

350g/12oz oyster, or medium cap, mushrooms
4 tbsp olive oil
3 garlic cloves, chopped
2.5cm/1inch fresh ginger root, finely chopped
1 tsp lightly crushed Szechuan peppercorns
1 tbsp sesame seeds

Serves 4

Gingered parsnip batons

INGREDIENTS

500g/1lb parsnips 2 tbsp olive oil
15g/½oz butter
5cm/2inch piece fresh root ginger, finely
shredded
1 tbsp lemon juice
½ tsp soft light brown sugar
salt and pepper to taste
snipped chives to garnish

METHOD

Cut the parsnips in half across the middle, then cut each piece lengthways into 4 or 6 pieces to give batons of approximately equal size. Heat the oil and butter in a wok or large frying pan. Add the ginger and parsnips and stir-fry for about 5 minutes, until the parsnips are tender.

Add the lemon juice and sugar to the pan and cook for about 1 minute until the parsnips are lightly glazed. Season with salt and pepper. Transfer to a warmed serving dish and sprinkle with snipped chives to serve.

Serves 4

Sesame seed prawn toasts

INGNCDICNTS

225g/8oz uncooked prawns, peeled
1 garlic clove, crushed
1 egg white, lightly beaten
1 tsp finely chopped spring onions
½ tsp finely chopped root ginger
1 tbsp cornflour paste
15ml/1 tbsp fish sauce
115-150g/4-5oz white sesame seeds
6 large slices white bread
vegetable oil for deep frying
salt and ground black pepper

METHOD

With a sharp knife, chop the prawns into small pieces then mix these together with the garlic, spring onions, ginger, sugar, salt and pepper, fish sauce and egg white to form a paste. Spread the sesame seeds evenly on a large plate or tray. Next, spread the prawn paste thickly on one side of each slice of bread, then press spread side down, on to the seeds

Heat the oil in a wok and then fry 2-3 slices of the sesame bread at a time (depending on the size of your wok), spread side down, for 2-3 minutes. Remove and drain any excess oil. Finally cut away the crusts from the bread and divide the remaining into eight fingers .

Crispy seaweed

METHOD

Cut off the hard stalks in the centre of each spring green leaf. Pile the leaves on top of each other, and roll into a tight sausage shape. Thinly cut the leaves into fine shreds. Spread them out to dry. Heat the oil in a wok until hot.

Deep fry the shredded greens in batches, stirring to separate them. Remove the greens with a slotted spoon as soon as they are crispy, but before they turn brown. Drain. Sprinkle the salt and sugar evenly all over the seaweed and mix well.

INGREDIENTS

450g/1lb spring greens
vegetable oil, for deep frying
½ tsp salt
1 tsp caster sugar

Sweet and sour noodles

METHOD

To make the sauce, mix all the ingredients together in a small bowl then set aside. Meanwhile, cook the noodles according to the packet instructions. Heat the oil in a wok and add the garlic, ginger, leek, carrot, baby corn and red pepper. Stir-fry over a high heat for 2 minutes.

Add the sauce to the vegetables and stir until thickened. Lower the heat and simmer for about 2 minutes. Drain the noodles and add to the wok with the tomato wedges and coriander. Toss gently and season. Serve immediately, garnished with coriander.

INGREDIENTS

250g/8oz thread egg noodles
3 tbsp groundnut oil
1 garlic clove, crushed
2.5cm/1inch piece fresh root ginger, grated
I small leek, sliced
1 carrot, cut into strips
125g/4oz baby corn cobs, halved
½ red pepper, cut into diamonds
2 tomatoes, cut into wedges
1 tbsp chopped coriander leaves
salt and pepper to taste
coriander sprigs to garnish

FOR THE SAUCE

3 tbsp soy sauce
3 tbsp wine vinegar
3 tbsp sherry
3 tbsp soft light brown sugar
6 tbsp pineapple juice
1 tsp cornflour

Chilli chicken with water chestnuts

Serves 2

METHOD

Chinese styles of cooking can be healthy as food is cooked quickly and with very little fat. The important thing to remember is that the oil in the wok must be hot before adding any ingredients so that they will start to cook immediately. However, if the oil is too hot and begins to smoke then remove from the heat and allow to cool, as food added at this stage will burn and become bitter.

Heat the oil in a wok and stir-fry the garlic, onions and ginger for about 10-15 seconds, and then add chicken, toss the wok, and continue cooking for about 5–8 minutes, until the chicken is cooked through. Stir in the chilli, soy sauce and honey, then the chestnuts and heat through. Serve with rice or noodles.

INGREDIENTS

15ml/1 tbsp groundnut oil
1 garlic clove, crushed
4 spring onions, sliced diagonally
2cm/1inch fresh ginger, grated
2 boneless chicken breasts, sliced
15ml/1 tbsp chilli sauce
30ml/2 tbsp light soy sauce
15ml/1 tbsp clear honey
220g/7½oz tinned water chestnuts, drained and sliced

Thai style fish kebabs

Serves 4

METHOD

Cut the fish into large chunks, place them in a food processor with the prawns and blend until finely chopped. Transfer the fish mixture to a bowl and combine with the lime rind, garlic, chilli, spring onions, water chestnuts and fish sauce. Divide and mould the mixture into 20 balls. Roll the balls in the chopped peanuts, then chill them for 1 hour.

Thread the fish balls on to the skewers (see page 25), brush them with oil and cook under a hot grill, for about 15-20 minutes, turning them during cooking. Serve garnished with coriander or lime wedges and accompanied by rice noodles.

INGREDIENTS

450g/1lb white fish fillets, skinned
175g/6oz peeled prawns (shrimp)
1 tsp grated lime rind
1 garlic clove, crushed
1 small red chilli, finely chopped
2 tbsp finely chopped spring onions
6 water chestnuts, finely chopped
1 tbsp fish sauce or light soy sauce
115g/4oz salted peanuts, chopped
oil for brushing
lime wedges or coriander for garnish

Pork with satay sauce

Serves 4-5

(see page 25)

METHOD

Thread the pork onto eight wooden skewers (see page 25) and lay in a shallow dish. Mix together the onion, soy sauce and sugar, pour over the pork, turning the meat to coat evenly. Cover the dish and leave for at least 1 hour. For the sauce, heat 1 tbsp oil over a high heat, add the peanuts and fry, stirring, for 2 minutes. Transfer to paper towels to drain. Mix the chillies, shallots, lemon grass, garlic and blachan to a paste.

Heat the remaining oil over a moderate heat, add the spice paste and fry, stirring for 2 minutes. Grind the nuts until smooth and stir into the paste. Gradually stir in the coconut milk and bring to the boil. Add the sugar and lime juice and simmer for 5-10 minutes, until thickened. Cover and keep warm over a very low heat.

Preheat the grill. Grill the pork for 4-5 minutes on each side. Place on a bed of salad leaves, and serve with sauce.

INGREDIENTS

575g 1¼ lb lean pork, cut into 1.25cm/ ½inch cubes
1 small onion, finely chopped
3 tbsp dark soy sauce
1 tsp dark muscovado sugar
salad leaves to serve

FOR THE SAUCE

4 tbsp peanut oil
85g/3oz peanuts
2 fresh red chillies, chopped
3 shallots, chopped
2 stalks lemon grass
2 garlic cloves, chopped
2.5cm/1inch piece blachan
300ml/½ pint/1½ cups coconut milk
2 tsp dark muscovado sugar
juice of ½ lime

Asian beef curls

Serves 2

METHOD

If necessary beat out the meat to a thickness of 2mm (⅙inch). Then cut it into ribbons 1.25cm (½inch) wide and about 10-12.5cm (4-5 inches long). Combine the ingredients for the marinade and pour it over the meat. Chill for 4 hours. Remove the meat from the marinade, drain it well, then roll it up. Thread the rolls on to the bamboo skewers (see page 25).

Put the marinade into a saucepan. Add the honey and water and boil for 2-3 minutes. Blend the cornflour with one tbsp water and stir this into the sauce. Simmer for 2 minutes to thicken. Brush the meat with a little oil and cook on a hot oiled griddle plate or the barbecue grill rack for 4-6 minutes, turning the skewers over once. Serve with the sauce, for dipping.

INGREDIENTS

6 thin slices quick-fry beef, about
400g/14oz
1 tbsp honey
150ml/¼ pint water
1 tsp cornflour
a little oil

FOR THE SPICY SOY MARINADE

3 tbsp light soy sauce
1 tbsp dark soy sauce
2 tbsp rice vinegar
2 garlic cloves , crushed
2 tsp chopped fresh ginger root
½ tsp five-spice powder
1 green chilli, seeded and chopped
1 red chilli, seeded and chopped
3 spring onions thinly sliced
3 tbsp beef stock

Chicken with black bean sauce

Serves 4

METHOD

In a bowl, mix together the sherry, black bean sauce, stock or water and cornflour until smooth. Heat half the oil in a wok and stir-fry the chicken briskly until sealed all over.

Remove from the wok and keep warm. Add the remaining oil to the wok. Add the spring onions, baby corn, mangetout, red pepper and garlic and stir-fry for 2 minutes. Return the chicken to the wok and add the cornflour mixture. Cook, stirring, until thickened. Turn on to a warmed serving dish and serve with Chinese noodles or rice.

INGREDIENTS

4 tbsp sherry
6 tbsp black bean sauce
4 tbsp chicken stock or water
1 tsp cornflour
3 tbsp groundnut oil
350g/12oz boneless chicken breasts, cut into thin strips
1 bunch spring onions, cut into 2.5cm/1inch lengths
125g/4oz baby corn cobs, halved lengthways
125g/4oz mangetout, topped and tailed
1 red pepper, cored, seeded and thinly sliced
2 garlic cloves, chopped

Vegetable stir-fry with peanut noodles

Serves 2

METHOD

In a blender, blend the peanuts, 15ml (1 tbsp) of the oil, vinegar, sugar and 15ml (1 tbsp) of the soy sauce with enough water to make a runny sauce. Set aside.

Cook the noodles according to·the packet instructions, drain and combine with the sauce. Heat the remaining oil and stir-fry the spring onions and garlic for 2 minutes. Add the vegetables and stir-fry for 5 minutes more. Combine the cornflour with the remaining soy and chilli sauce or ketchup. Stir this into the vegetables with a little water if necessary.

Pile the vegetables on top of the noodles and serve. Cornflour needs to be mixed or 'slackened' with a small amount of water before it is combined with other ingredients to prevent it forming lumps.

INGREDIENTS

4 spring onions, diagonally sliced
2 garlic cloves, finely sliced
500g/1lb 2oz mixed vegetables of choice
(e.g. peppers, carrots, broccoli, cabbage,
beans, mangetout, mushrooms)
45ml/3 tbsp soy sauce
15ml/1 tbsp chilli sauce or ketchup
2 tsp cornflour, mixed with 15ml/1 tbsp
of water
250g/8oz egg or rice noodles
55g/1½oz peanuts, shelled and skinned
30ml/2 tbsp groundnut oil
15ml/1 tbsp white wine or rice vinegar
1 tsp sugar

Swordfish kebabs with coriander noodles

Serves 4

METHOD

Set a large pan of salted water to boil. Remove any skin and dark meat from the fish and cut into cubes of about 2cm (1inch). Wash the courgettes and tomatoes and cut the courgettes into thick rounds. Skewer the fish with the vegetables alternately until the skewer is full.

Peel and grate the ginger and the garlic. Mix with a tbsp of oil, the lime juice and seasoning. Place the kebabs on a grill pan and pour over the oil marinade. Grill the kebabs under a hot grill, turning occasionally for 8–10 minutes.

Meanwhile, place the noodles in boiling water, remove from the heat and allow to stand for 4–5 minutes. Stir well then drain and toss them with the coriander. Serve the kebabs on a bed of noodles and dress with light soy sauce.

INGREDIENTS

450g/1lb swordfish
230g/8oz courgettes
230g/8oz cherry tomatoes
1 tsp grated fresh ginger
1 garlic clove
1 tbsp lime juice
fresh or dried coriander
250g/9oz thread egg noodles
vegetable oil
light soy sauce
salt and pepper

Spicy pork chops

Serves 4

METHOD

Using a pestle and mortar or small blender, mix the basil, garlic, ginger and chillies to a paste then stir in the soy sauce. Rub the spice mixture into the pork, place in a shallow non-metal dish, cover and leave at room temperature for 1 hour, or in a cool place for 3 hours.

Preheat the grill. Grill the pork chops for 8-10 minutes on each side, basting with the cooking juices occasionally. Delicious served with rice or noodles.

INGREDIENTS

2 tbsp finely chopped basil
2 tbsp finely chopped garlic
2 tbsp grated ginger root
2 tbsp finely chopped fresh green chillies
2 tbsp soy sauce
4 pork chops

Sizzling beef

INGREDIENTS

450g/1lb rump or sirloin steak
1½ tsp sesame oil
2 tsp rice wine or dry sherry
1½ tsp light soy sauce
1½ tsp cornfllour
1 egg white
125ml/4fl oz peanut oil
3 fresh red chillies, shredded
10 spring onions, cut into 2.5cm/1inch
pieces
1 small garlic clove, finely chopped
2 tsp finely chopped ginger root
1½ tsp chilli bean sauce
1 tsp bean sauce
4 tsp oyster sauce

Serves 4

METHOD

Put the beef into the freezer for 20 minutes, until firm to the touch, then slice very thinly across the grain. Mix together sesame oil, rice wine or sherry, soy sauce, cornflour and egg white. Add the beef and leave for 20-30 minutes. Heat a wok until very hot, add the peanut oil and the beef, stirring to separate the slices for 1 minute.

Using a slotted spoon, transfer the beef to paper towels. Remove all except 2 tbsp of oil from the wok. Add the chillies, spring onions, garlic, ginger, chilli bean sauce and bean sauce. Stir-fry for 30 seconds, add 2 tbsp of water and the oyster sauce, simmer for 30 seconds, then return the beef to the wok. Serve sizzling hot.

Tofu, yellow bean sauce and mangetout stir-fry

Serves 2

METHOD

Heat the sunflower oil in a wok. When the oil is very hot, cook the sliced onion and carrots for about 5 minutes, stirring continuously until they begin to soften. Add the tofu and yellow bean sauce to the wok, then cook for a further 10 minutes. Both these products are widely available from major supermarkets and ethnic food shops.

Stir in the mangetout and cook for about 2-3 minutes. Remove from the wok and serve with rice or noodles. Stir-fries like this one can also be served as a tasty filling for jacket potatoes.

INGREDIENTS

1 tbsp sunflower oil
1 large onion, thinly sliced
110g/4oz carrots, sliced on the diagonal
230g/8oz firm tofu
½ jar yellow bean sauce
110g/4oz mangetout
rice or noodles to serve

Chinese duck soup

Serves 4

METHOD

Soak the noodles in boiling water to cover for 10 minutes, then drain. Heat the oil in a pan, add the duck strips and fry briskly for 1-2 minutes. Add the mushrooms, spring onions, garlic and baby corn and stir-fry for 1-2 minutes.

Add the stock, noodles, soy sauce and seasoning. Bring to the boil and simmer for 1 minute. Add the pak choi and sesame oil and simmer for about 2 minutes. Serve immediately.

INGREDIENTS

50g/2oz thin rice stick noodles, broken into pieces
2 tbsp groundnut oil
2 boneless duck breasts, skinned and cut into thin strips
125g/4oz shiitake mushrooms, thinly sliced
4 spring onions, diagonally sliced
2 garlic cloves, sliced
175g/6oz baby corn cobs, halved lengthways
1.2 litres/2 pints chicken or duck stock
2 tbsp soy sauce
salt and pepper to taste
125g/4oz pak choi, shredded
1 tsp sesame oil

Mussels with black bean sauce

Serves 2

250ml/8fl oz white wine
2 garlic cloves, sliced
15g/½oz fresh parsley, chopped
1kg/2lb 2oz fresh mussels, scrubbed
and debearded
250g/8oz egg noodles or spaghetti
45ml/3 tbsp black bean sauce
1 tsp cornflour, mixed with 15ml/1tbsp
water
15ml/1tbsp soy sauce

METHOD

Mussels are cheap, high in iron, and not as much hassle to prepare as they might seem. To clean mussels, rinse or scrub them in cold water and remove the clump of hair (the 'beard') by pulling downwards with a sharp tug.

Bring the wine to the boil in a large pot with about 1cm (½inch) of water. Add the garlic, the mussels and half of the parsley, and cover. Steam for 4–5 minutes – the shells should be open. Remove the open mussels and cover for about 1 more minute. Remove all the mussels, discarding the unopened ones.

Remove the flesh from the inside of the mussels, set aside. Cook the noodles according to the packet instructions. Strain the mussel/wine juice into a smaller pan and bring to the boil. Stir in the black bean sauce, soy sauce and cornflour and cook for about 1 minute until thickened. Stir in the mussels and serve over the drained noodles, garnished with parsley.

Beef, red pepper and beansprout stir-fry

Serves 4

METHOD

Heat the sunflower oil in a wok or large frying pan until very hot, then carefully add the sliced onion. Stir with a wooden spoon for about 3 minutes, until soft, then add the steak strips and cook for a further 5 minutes.

Meanwhile, cook the noodles, following the instructions on the packet. Add the peppers and beansprouts to the wok or frying pan, and stir-fry for a further 3 minutes until the vegetables are cooked. Stir in the rice wine, add salt and black pepper to taste and heat through to serve. Place the cooked, drained noodles on a plate and top with the stir-fry.

INGREDIENTS

1 tbsp sunflower oil
1 large onion, sliced
340g/12oz steak, cut into
thin strips
2 red peppers, thinly sliced
110g/4oz beansprouts
2 tbsp rice wine
noodles to serve

和愛寿

Aromatic lamb

Serves 4

METHOD

Crush together the cumin and coriander seeds. Mix with the mustard, lime juice, tahini, garlic, chilli powder and salt, then slowly pour in the oil, stirring. Put the lamb into a shallow dish and spread evenly with the spicy mixture.

Cover and leave at room temperature for 2 hours, or refrigerate overnight. On the day of serving, stir together the dip ingredients. Cover and chill lightly.

If the lamb has been refrigerated, return to room temperature 30-40 minutes before cooking. Preheat the grill. When the grill is very hot, cook the lamb until blackened in patches (5-8 minutes on each side). Turn off the grill and leave the lamb to rest for about 5 minutes. Serve thickly sliced with the dip.

INGREDIENTS

1 tsp roasted cumin seeds
1 tbsp coriander seeds
1 tbsp wholegrain mustard
1½ tbsp lime juice
1 tbsp tahini
2 garlic cloves, finely chopped
¼-½ tsp chilli powder
salt
2 tbsp olive oil
2 lamb neck fillets, about 350g/12oz each

FOR THE CHILLI DIP

handful of coriander leaves, finely chopped
¼-½ tsp chilli powder
salt
150g/5oz Greek yoghurt

Serves 4

Chilli corn cobs with tomato

INGREDIENTS

2 tbsp groundnut oil
2 tsp sesame oil
1 garlic clove, crushed
2.5cm/1inch piece fresh root ginger, grated
250g/8oz baby corn cobs
2 tbsp sweet chilli sauce
1 tbsp light soy sauce
1 tbsp sherry
1 tsp sugar
4 tomatoes, skinned and cut into wedges
4 spring onions, shredded
salt and pepper to taste

METHOD

This is simply delicious and very very easy to make. The strong flavour makes this an ideal accompaniment to plain grilled chicken or fish. Heat the oils in a wok then add the garlic, ginger and corn cobs and stir-fry for about 3 minutes.

Add the remaining ingredients and stir-fry for 2-3 minutes, until the corn cobs are tender. Add seasoning and serve immediately.

Serves 4

Black bean and vegetable stir-fry

INGREDIENTS

8 spring onions
225g/8oz button mushrooms
1 red pepper
1 green pepper
2 large carrots
60ml/4 tbsp black bean sauce
90ml/6 tbsp warm water
225g/8oz beansprouts
salt and ground black pepper

METHOD

With a sharp knife, thinly slice the onions and mushrooms. Cut both the peppers in half, remove the seeds and slice the flesh into thin strips. Next, cut the carrots in half. Cut each half into thin strips lengthways then stack the slices and cut through them to make very fine strips. Heat the oil in the wok until very hot then add the spring onions and garlic and stir-fry for 30 seconds.

Add the mushrooms, peppers and carrots. Stir-fry for 5-6 minutes over a high heat until the vegetables are just beginning to soften. Mix the black bean sauce with the water then add to the wok and continue to cook for another 3-4 minutes. Finally, stir in the beansprouts and cook for 1 minute more, until all the vegetables are coated in the sauce.

Fragrant Thai meatballs

METHOD

To make the sauce, place the oil in a small saucepan, add the curry paste and fry for about a minute. Add the peanut butter, palm sugar, lemon juice and coconut milk and stir thoroughly. Continue to stir and bring the sauce to the boil. Lower the heat and simmer for about 5 minutes, or until the sauce thickens. For the meatballs, combine all the ingredients, except for the rice flour, oil and coriander. In a food processor or blender, mix thoroughly. Dust your hands with rice flour, then shape the mixture into small balls, and dust the meatballs with rice flour. Heat the oil in a wok until hot and deep fry the meatballs in batches until nicely browned and cooked through.

INGREDIENTS

450g/1lb lean minced pork or beef
1 tbsp chopped garlic
1 stalk lemon grass, finely chopped
4 spring onions, finely chopped
1 tbsp chopped fresh coriander
2 tbsp red curry paste
15ml/1 tbsp lemon juice
15ml/1 tbsp fish sauce
1 egg
salt and freshly ground black pepper
rice flour for dusting
oil for frying
sprigs of coriander, to garnish

FOR THE PEANUT SAUCE

15ml/1 tbsp vegetable oil
1 tbsp red curry paste
2 tbsp crunchy peanut butter
1 tbsp palm sugar
15ml/1 tbsp lemon juice
250ml/8fl oz coconut milk

Sizzling trout with garlic and spring onions

METHOD

Wash the trout and remove the heads. Using a sharp knife, make 2 or 3 slashes through the skin on each side of the fish. Heat 15g (½oz) of the butter and 1 tbsp of oil in a large frying pan. Add the trout and fry for about 4 minutes on each side until just cooked. Transfer to a plate and keep hot.

Add the rest of the butter and oil to the pan. Add the garlic, ginger and spring onions and stir-fry for 1 minute, then stir in the remaining ingredients and return the trout to the pan. Cook for one minute over a high heat until hot and sizzling. Serve at once, garnished with lemon wedges.

INGREDIENTS

2 Trout, cleaned
25g/1 oz butter
2 tbsp virgin olive oil
2 garlic cloves, thinly sliced
½ tbsp grated fresh root ginger
4 spring onions, sliced
1 tbsp chopped parsley
juice of ½ lemon
¼ tsp finely grated lemon rind
salt and pepper to taste
Lemon wedges to garnish

Five-spice chicken breasts

Serves 4

Put the marinade ingredients into a bowl and stir until the sugar dissolves. Place the chicken breasts in a glass dish, pour over the marinade and chill for 1-4 hours, turning the portions over halfway.

Place the chicken breasts on an oiled grill rack underneath a hot grill (ensuring there is a dish underneath to catch any drips) and cook them for about 8 minutes on each side (or longer for larger pieces), brushing them with the marinade during cooking. Transfer to a chopping board, leave to stand for 2 minutes, then cut them lengthways into slices and arrange the slices on warmed serving plates. Garnish with a few shreds of red and yellow peppers.

INGREDIENTS

4 boneless chicken breasts
¼ red and ¼ yellow pepper, finely shredded, for garnish

FOR THE FIVE-SPICE MARINADE

5 tbsp light soy sauce
5 tbsp dark soy sauce
5 tbsp dry sherry
2 tsp brown sugar
1 tsp five-spice powder
2 garlic cloves, crushed
¼ tsp cayenne pepper
1 tbsp grated fresh ginger root

和愛寿

Spicy tofu with corn

Serves 2

METHOD

Tofu is an ingredient many people have had negative experiences with because of its bland taste ... a disadvantage in itself but a distinct advantage when cooked with other strong flavours as it soaks them right up.

Combine together the soy sauce, honey, chilli and vinegar in a bowl. Drain and cut the tofu into 1cm (½inch) cubes and stir into the marinade. Leave to marinate for 15 minutes. Heat the oil in a wok or frying pan and stir-fry the spring onions, garlic, ginger and corn for about 3 minutes. Add the tofu and marinade with the yellow bean sauce, then stir in the cornflour with about 15ml (1fl oz) of water to make a sauce. Cook for 1 minute and serve over noodles or rice, sprinkled with the sesame seeds.

INGREDIENTS

330g/11oz firm tofu
30ml/2 tbsp soy sauce
15ml/1 tbsp clear honey
15ml/1 tbsp chilli sauce
15ml/1 tbsp rice, sherry or white wine vinegar
30ml/2 tbsp groundnut oil
4 spring onions, sliced diagonally
2 garlic cloves, crushed
3cm/1½inch piece fresh ginger, shredded
250g/8oz baby corn, with the ends trimmed off
15ml/1 tbsp yellow bean sauce
1 tsp cornflour
toasted sesame seeds (optional)

Fragrant roast pork

Serves 6-8

Put the pork into a shallow, non-metal dish. Mix together the peppers, peppercorns, cinnamon, cloves, fennel seeds, turmeric and salt. Rub evenly into the pork, cover and leave in a cool place for at least 4 hours, or refrigerate overnight. In a blender, combine the sesame oil, peanut oil and lemon and orange zests. Set aside. If the pork has been refrigerated, return to room temperature 30 minutes before cooking. Rub the pork with the oil mixture.

Preheat the oven to 180°C/350°F/Gas Mark 4. Roast the pork for about 1¼ hours, turning every 10 minutes or so and basting with any cooking juices and remaining oil mixture, until a skewer inserted in the centre comes out clean. Leave to stand for 20 minutes before slicing. Spoon the cooking juices over the slices and garnish with coriander leaves.

INGREDIENTS

1.4kg/3lb boned, rolled and tied pork loin
2-3 tsp black pepper
1½ tsp white pepper
1½ tbsp szechuan peppercorns, ground
1½ tbsp green peppercorns
¾ tsp ground cinnamon
½ tsp ground cloves
2 tsp finely crushed fennel seeds
½ tsp turmeric
salt
1½ tbsp sesame oil
3 tbsp peanut oil
1½ tbsp grated lemon zest
2 tbsp grated orange zest
coriander leaves, to garnish

Chicken, pak choi and bamboo shoot stir-fry

Serves 4

INGREDIENTS

**1tbsp sunflower oil
1 large onion, finely sliced
230g/8oz tinned bamboo
shoots, drained
230g/8oz tinned water
chestnuts, drained
170g/6oz pak choi
340g/12oz chicken breast
2 tbsp soy sauce
salt and ground black pepper
boiled noodles or rice to serve
flat-leaf parsley to garnish**

METHOD

Heat the sunflower oil in a wok or large frying pan, then add the finely sliced onion. Cook for about 3 minutes, stirring continuously until soft but not browned. Drain the bamboo shoots and water chestnuts.

Wash, trim and chop the pak choi. Cut the chicken breasts into thin strips. Add the chicken and pak choi to the wok and cook for a further 5 minutes, or until the chicken is cooked through, stirring continuously. Add the drained bamboo shoots and water chestnuts and soy sauce, then stir until heated through. Add a small amount of salt (you may not need much due to the soy sauce) and pepper to taste and serve with either noodles or rice.

Brown rice with soy sauce and green vegetables

Serves 2

METHOD

Cook the brown rice according to the packet instructions. Meanwhile, cook the peas and the broccoli until tender. When the rice is ready, mix in the peas and broccoli and stir in the spring onions. Add a dash of soy sauce to taste and serve immediately.

This dish can also be served cold as a side salad. You can, of course, add your own variation of vegetables if you choose. Finely chopped mangetout and green beans are a good option, but you can use whatever you have in your store cupboard.

INGREDIENTS

110g/4oz brown rice
110g/4oz frozen peas
110g/4oz broccoli, cut into florets
3 spring onions, chopped
soy sauce, to taste

Oriental chicken salad

Serves 4

METHOD

Blanch the mangetout and baby corn in boiling water for 3 minutes. Drain and rinse under cold water, then drain thoroughly. Place in a bowl with the chicken, spring onions, red pepper and mushrooms. Toss to mix.

To make the dressing, put the sesame paste in a bowl and gradually mix in the vinegar and sherry. Add the soy sauce, sesame oil and garlic and mix together thoroughly, adding seasoning to taste.

Pour the dressing over the salad, toss well and sprinkle with the nuts to serve.

INGREDIENTS

250g/8oz mangetout, topped and tailed
250g/8oz baby corn, halved lengthways
350g/12oz cooked chicken, cut into strips
4 spring onions, thinly sliced
1 red pepper, cored, seeded and cut into strips
125g/4oz mushrooms, sliced
25g/1oz cashew nuts, toasted

FOR THE DRESSING

2 tbsp tahini
2 tbsp rice or wine vinegar
2 tbsp medium dry sherry
1 tbsp soy sauce
1 tsp sesame oil
1 garlic clove, crushed
salt and pepper to taste

Oriental pork fillet

METHOD

Place the pork fillet in a shallow dish. Combine the marinade ingredients and pour over the pork. Turn the meat so that it is well coated and leave to marinade for at least 2 hours, turning the pork every 20 minutes. Put all the ingredients for the chilli sauce in a food processor and blend until the chilli is finely chopped. Transfer to a bowl, cover and chill overnight.

Place the pork on the prepared barbecue and cook, over a medium heat, turning and brushing with the marinade for 20-25 minutes. Once it is seared all over, move it to a cooler section of the barbecue to complete cooking. To serve, cut the pork across the grain into 5mm (¼inch) thick slices and arrange on a serving platter accompanied by the chilli sauce and fried noodles.

INGREDIENTS

450-675g/1-1½lb pork fillet

FOR THE MARINADE

5cm/2inch piece fresh ginger root, finely chopped
2 tbsp dark soy sauce
2 tbsp peanut (groundnut) oil
2 tbsp hoisin sauce
1 tbsp honey

FOR THE CHILLI DIPPING SAUCE

2 tbsp oil
1 garlic clove, crushed
2 tbsp light brown sugar
1 small red chilli
3 tbsp dark soy sauce
2 tbsp plum jam

Cantonese turkey steaks

Serves 4

METHOD

Put all the ingredients for the spice paste
into a bowl and mix them together well.
Brush the turkey steaks with the paste,
place them in a glass dish, cover and
chill for at least 2 hours, or overnight.

When ready to cook, brush the turkey
steaks with a little oil, place them under
a hot grill and cook them for about 10-
12 minutes (depending on the thickness
of the steaks), turning them over halfway.
Serve with noodles and stir-fried
vegetables.

INGREDIENTS

4 turkey breast steaks, about
175g/6oz each
a little oil

FOR THE CHINESE SPICE PASTE

2 tsp sugar
½ tsp five-spice powder
½ tsp garlic salt
¼ tsp chilli powder
1 tsp paprika
1 tsp malt vinegar
1 tsp tomato purée

Malaysian chicken packages

Serves 4

INGREDIENTS

**4 boneless, skinless chicken breasts
with wing
2 tbsp chopped fresh coriander**

FOR THE COCONUT MARINADE

**55g/2oz creamed coconut
85ml/3fl oz water
1 red pepper, coarsely chopped
1 tbsp chopped fresh lemon grass
1 garlic clove, crushed
1 red chilli, seeded and chopped
3 spring onions, chopped
2.5cm/1inch piece fresh ginger root,
coarsely chopped**

METHOD

Put the creamed coconut into a pan with
the water and heat gently, stirring until it
dissolves. Pour into a food processor,
add the remaining marinade ingredients
and blend until smooth. Leave to cool.
Place the chicken portions in a glass
dish, pour over the marinade and chill for
1-4 hours, turning the portions over
halfway. Lift the chicken from the
marinade and place each portion on a
piece of double thickness foil, large
enough to enclose the chicken. Spoon
over the marinade and sprinkle with the
coriander.

Wrap the foil around the chicken to form
a package, sealing all the edges to
ensure that it does not leak during the
cooking. Place the packages under a
hot grill and cook for 20-25 minutes,
keeping the seam at the top so the
juices do not run out. Serve the chicken
with the juices and accompanied by
boiled fragrant rice.

Tofu with broccoli and pork

Serves 2

METHOD

This is a classic and very tasty combination, and the tofu bumps up the amount of protein without adding extra saturated fat.

Heat the oil in a wok or large frying pan and stir-fry the onions, garlic and pork for 5 minutes. Add the tofu and broccoli. Mix together the remaining ingredients and stir into the wok. Add a little water if necessary to steam the broccoli if it is cooking at a slower rate than the other ingredients. Continue to stir-fry for 5 minutes then serve over rice or noodles.

INGREDIENTS

15ml/1 tbsp groundnut oil
4 spring onions, sliced
2 garlic cloves, crushed
100g/3½oz lean pork mince
200g/6½oz firm tofu, drained, patted dry and cut into 2cm/1inch cubes
250g/8oz broccoli, in bite-sized pieces
30ml/2 tbsp soy sauce
15ml/1 tbsp white wine or rice vinegar
1 tbsp sugar
30ml/2 tbsp hoisin sauce

Chicken noodle salad

Serves 2

METHOD

This is a great recipe for using up left-over roast chicken. Alternatively you can poach or grill a couple of breasts for this tasty and refreshing salad.

Combine the dressing ingredients together and mix briskly with a fork. Allow to stand for about 10-15 minutes to allow the flavours to fuse. Cook the noodles according to the packet instructions, drain. Hold the noodles in the colander under the cold water tap and run the water over them to refresh. Drain well and place to one side. Cut the carrot and courgette into matchsticks or ribbons using a vegetable peeler or sharp knife. Combine these with the spring onions, noodles, chicken, dressing and coriander and sprinkle with the sesame seeds.

INGREDIENTS

250g/8oz egg or rice noodles
4 spring onions, shredded
1 carrot, julienned
1 courgette, julienned
330g/11oz cooked chicken, shredded
toasted sesame seeds (optional)
15g/½oz coriander, chopped

THE DRESSING

1 garlic clove, crushed
15ml/1 tbsp rice or white wine vinegar
15ml/1 tbsp lemon juice
15ml/1 tbsp clear honey
15ml/1 tbsp chilli sauce
30ml/2 tbsp groundnut oil
5ml/1 tsp sesame seed oil (optional)

Chicken satay

Serves 2

METHOD

Cut the chicken into 2cm (¾inch) cubes. Mix together all the ingredients for the marinade in a bowl. Add the chicken and rub the marinade into the meat. Cover and chill for up to 24 hours.

Put the creamed coconut in a bowl with 150ml (¼pint) of water and stir until it dissolves. Heat the oil in a small saucepan, add the shallots and garlic and cook until they are soft. Stir in the coconut milk, chilli powder, peanut butter, sugar and soy sauce and continue stirring over a gentle heat for about 3 minutes. Keep the sauce warm.

Thread the chicken cubes on to the skewers (see page 25). Place them on a prepared barbecue and cook until browned (about 6-8 minutes), brushing with a little oil during cooking. Serve with the peanut sauce.

INGREDIENTS

450g/1 lb boned, skinless chicken

FOR THE SATAY MARINADE

2 tbsp oil
½ tsp chilli powder
2 tsp ground coriander
2 tsp ground cumin
1 garlic clove, crushed
1 tbsp dark soy sauce
2 tbsp lime juice
1 tbsp brown sugar

FOR THE PEANUT SAUCE

3 tbsp creamed coconut
2 tbsp oil
2 shallots, finely chopped
1 garlic clove, crushed
½ tsp chilli powder
3 tbsp smooth peanut butter
2 tsp dark brown sugar
1 tsp dark soy sauce

Chicken with szechuan peppercorns

Serves 3-4

METHOD

Cut the chicken into strips then heat the peanut oil in a large frying pan or wok. Add the chicken and stir-fry for about 3 minutes. Next add the peppercorns, spring onions, garlic, ginger, shrimp paste, chillies, rice wine and soy sauce.

Continue to stir-fry for a further 3 minutes until the chicken is cooked through yet tender. Remove from the wok and then sprinkle the chicken with sesame oil.

Serve immediately on a bed of noodles. Try the Scented lemon noodles on page 22.

INGREDIENTS

700g/1½lb chicken thighs
1½ tbsp peanut oil

FOR THE SAUCE

1 tsp roasted Szechuan peppercorns,
ground
4 tsp finely chopped spring onion
1 garlic clove, finely chopped
2 tsp grated ginger
1-1¼ tsp shrimp paste
2 fresh red chillies, chopped
1½ tsp rice wine or dry sherry
1¼ tsp dark soy sauce
few drops of sesame oil

Prawn and egg stir-fried rice

Serves 2

METHOD

If you cannot buy fresh prawns or shrimp, you can use frozen but make sure you defrost thoroughly before you start cooking. Beat the eggs gently in a cup or small bowl with a seasoning of salt and pepper.

Heat a small frying pan, add the butter and when it foams, pour in the egg mixture. Cook over a medium heat, tilting the pan so that any runny egg mixture is evenly distributed. Cook until the egg is set, then flip the omelette to cook the underside. Slide the omelette on to a chopping board and slice into thin strips. Cook the rice, drain and set aside. Heat the oil in a wok, then stir in the garlic and the spring onions and stir-fry for 2 minutes. Add the prawns and stir for 1-2 minutes to heat through. Add the cooked rice and stir again, then the strips of omelette.

INGREDIENTS

2 eggs
salt and freshly ground black pepper
knob of butter
110g/4oz white rice
1 tbsp sunflower oil
1 garlic clove, finely chopped
3 spring onions, finely chopped
170g/6oz cooked peeled prawns or shrimp,
defrosted if frozen
soy sauce (optional)

Serves 4

Chilli pork

INGREDIENTS

3 tbsp groundnut oil
625g/1¼ lb pork fillet (tenderloin), cubed
1 small onion, chopped
1 garlic clove, crushed
2.5cm/1inch piece fresh root ginger, grated
2 tsp mild chilli powder
½ tsp paprika
2 thyme sprigs
1 tbsp plain flour
2 tbsp tomato purée
150ml/¼ pint hot stock
salt and pepper to taste
Herb sprigs to garnish

METHOD

Heat the oil in a wok or sauté pan. Add the pork and stir-fry for 1-2 minutes to seal. Add the onion, garlic, ginger, chilli powder, paprika and thyme and continue stir-frying for 2 minutes, or until the onion is softened.

Add the flour to the pan and cook for 2 minutes, stirring occasionally. Stir in the tomato purée and remove from the heat. Gradually stir in the stock. Return to the heat and cook, stirring constantly, until the sauce is smooth and thickened. Cover and cook gently for 15 minutes. Discard the thyme and check the seasoning before serving, garnished with herbs.

Serves 4-6

Singapore noodles

INGREDIENTS

250g/8oz medium egg noodles
3 tbsp groundnut oil
1 tsp sesame oil
1 garlic clove, crushed
1 carrot, thinly sliced
50g/2oz cooked ham, cut into strips
75g/3oz peeled prawns
75g/3oz frozen petits pois, thawed
6 peeled water chestnuts, sliced
3 spring onions, sliced
50g/2oz beansprouts
125ml/4fl oz chicken stock
2 tbsp soy sauce
2 tsp cornflour
salt and pepper to taste

METHOD

Cook the egg noodles according to the packet instructions. Meanwhile, heat the oils in a wok. Add the garlic and carrot and stir-fry for 2 minutes. Add the ham, prawns, peas, water chestnuts, spring onions and beansprouts and stir-fry for 1 minute. Stir in the chicken stock and soy sauce and bring to the boil.

Blend the cornflour with 2 tbsp cold water and add to the wok. Cook, stirring, until thickened. Drain the noodles thoroughly and add to the wok. Heat through, tossing well. Season and serve at once.

Green vegetable stir-fry

METHOD

Slice the cucumber into batons and set aside. Heat the oils in a wok then add the garlic and ginger and stir-fry for a few seconds. Grate the bulb end only of the lemon grass, if using, and add to the wok with the broccoli, courgette, mangetout and the spring onions. Stir well and continue to cook for another 2-3 minutes.

Add the cucumber batons to the wok and stir-fry for a few seconds to heat through. Season with salt and pepper and serve at once.

INGREDIENTS

½ cucumber
3 tbsp groundnut oil
1 tsp sesame oil
½ garlic clove, crushed
2.5cm/1inch piece fresh root ginger, grated
1 stalk lemon grass (optional)
250g/8oz broccoli florets, halved
1 courgette, thinly sliced
125g/4oz mangetout
3 spring onions, shredded
salt and pepper to taste

Mushroom and nut fried rice

METHOD

If using the dried mushrooms, soak in boiling water to cover for 20 minutes. Drain, reserving 5 tbsp water. Discard the stalks and slice the mushroom caps. Heat the oil in a wok. Add the onion, button mushrooms, garlic and ginger and stir-fry for 2 minutes. Add the mangetout, red pepper and Chinese mushrooms, if using, and stir-fry for 1 minute.

Add the rice and nuts to the wok, together with the soy sauce, enough of the reserved mushroom liquid (or water) to moisten, and seasoning. Heat through, stirring to prevent sticking and serve garnished with coriander.

INGREDIENTS

5 dried Chinese mushrooms (optional)
3 tbsp groundnut or olive oil
1 small onion, chopped
175g/6oz button mushrooms, halved
1 garlic clove, crushed
2.5cm/1inch fresh root ginger, grated
50g/2oz mangetout
½ red pepper, cored, seeded and cut into thin strips
250g/8oz brown rice, cooked
40g/1½oz Brazil nuts, sliced
50g/2oz salted cashews
3 tbsp light soy sauce
salt and pepper to taste
coriander sprigs to garnish

Bankok beef

METHOD

Dissolve the creamed coconut in 3 tbsp of boiling water. Place in a food processor with the remaining curry paste ingredients and blend to a paste. Spread the paste over the beef. Cover and chill for at least 2 hours or overnight.

Grill the beef under a hot grill for about 20 minutes, brushing with a little oil and turning it over halfway. When it is cooked cut the steak into slices, against the grain of the meat and serve garnished with some shredded radish, cucumber and spring onions.

INGREDIENTS

1 piece rump steak 4cm/1½inch thick, about 450g/1lb
a little oil
shredded radish and spring onion for garnish

FOR THE THAI CURRY PASTE

3 tbsp creamed coconut
1 shallot
1 garlic clove
5cm/2inch piece lemon grass
2 tsp ground coriander
½ tsp ground cumin
½ tsp ground turmeric
½ tsp ground galangal
6 dried red chillies, seeded
salt and freshly ground black pepper
1 tsp grated lime rind

Scallops with lime

Serves 3-4

METHOD

Place the scallops on their shells in a steaming basket. Heat the oil in a frying pan, add the garlic and shallot and cook, stirring occasionally, until softened. Add the ginger and chilli, stir for 1 minute. Sprinkle over the scallops in the steaming basket and season with black pepper. Cover, place over a saucepan of boiling water and steam for 6-8 minutes until the scallops just begin to turn opaque.

In a small saucepan, gently heat the lime juice, sugar and fish sauce until the sugar dissolves. Transfer the scallops on their shells to a serving plate, spoon over lime sauce and scatter coriander on top. Serve immediately.

INGREDIENTS

12 scallops on the half shell
1 tbsp vegetable oil
2 garlic cloves, chopped
1 shallot, finely chopped
5mm/⅕inch fresh ginger root, finely chopped
1½ tsp finely chopped fresh red chilli
freshly ground black pepper
3 tbsp lime juice
¼ tsp sugar
1 tsp fish sauce
shredded coriander leaves, to garnish

Turkey chow mein

Serves 2

METHOD

Bring a pan of water to the boil, then cook the noodles, according to the instructions on the packet. Rinse in cold water and drain well.

Heat the oil in a wok or large frying pan then add the garlic and ginger. Cook for about a minute and then add the turkey. Cook for a further 3 minutes, then toss in the beansprouts, spring onions and red pepper. Toss the pan and cook for 1 more minute. Finally, add the chilli sauce, soy sauce and noodles and fry for about 3 minutes.

INGREDIENTS

125g/4½oz egg noodles
15ml/1 tbsp groundnut oil
2 garlic cloves, sliced
2.5cm/1inch piece root ginger, grated
2 turkey breasts, skinned and sliced
4 spring onions, diagonally sliced
100g/3½oz beansprouts
1 red pepper, finely sliced
15ml/1 tbsp chilli sauce
15ml/1 tbsp soy sauce

Stir-fried chicken, peppers and cashew nuts in yellow bean sauce

Serves 4-6

INGREDIENTS

2x250g/9oz packets of thread egg noodles
450g/1lb skinless chicken breast
110g/4oz cashew nuts
1 red and 1 yellow pepper
1 jar yellow bean sauce
2 tbsp vegetable oil
1 garlic clove, crushed
salt and pepper

METHOD

Place the noodles in a pan of boiling, salted water. Remove the pan from the heat immediately and leave to stand for 4–5 minutes, then drain. Meanwhile, thinly slice the chicken and deseed and thinly slice the peppers.

Heat the oil in the wok then add the chicken strips and stir vigorously. Cook for 2–3 minutes. Add the peppers and cook for 3 minutes more, still stirring. Add the garlic and cashews and cook until the chicken is tender and the peppers are cooked but not too soft. Add the yellow bean sauce and heat through. Check and adjust the seasoning. Serve on a bed of noodles.

Thai sweet potato and spinach curry

Serves 2

METHOD

Thai curries are delicious made with almost any vegetable, but this combination of sweet potato and spinach works particularly well. Coconut cream makes this curry extra good, but is high in fat, so only a small amount is used.

Place the chopped curry paste ingredients in a blender or food processor and process into a paste, adding more oil if necessary. Chop the sweet potatoes and potato into 2cm (1inch) cubes. Heat a wok or large saucepan and add 45–60ml (3–4 tbsp) of the curry paste with the sweet potato and potato then stir-fry for 3 minutes (if it sticks add a little of the stock).

Next add the stock and simmer part covered for 20 minutes until the potatoes are tender. Stir in the coconut milk and salt to taste and bring back to simmer. Stir in the spinach and cook for 1 more minute. Serve with rice or noodles.

THE CURRY PASTE

30ml/2 tbsp groundnut oil
10 shallots, peeled
2 garlic cloves, crushed
1–2 red chillies, deseeded
3cm/1½inch fresh ginger, peeled
2 stems of lemon grass, peeled
1 bunch of coriander

THE CURRY

2 large sweet potatoes
1 large potato
500ml/18fl oz vegetable stock
200ml/6½fl oz coconut milk
225g/7½oz spinach, washed
salt

Butterflied king prawns

Serves 4

METHOD

Remove the heads and fine legs from the prawns, but do not remove the tails. Using sharp scissors, cut the prawns lengthways almost in half, leaving the tails intact. Put in a shallow, non-metal dish. Whisk together the remaining ingredients, pour over the prawns, cover and leave in a cool place, turning occasionally, for 30-60 minutes.

Preheat the grill. Drain the prawns and thread onto four skewers (see page 25). Grill for 3-4 minutes on each side, basting occasionally with the spice mixture, until just cooked. Serve with any remaining spice mixture.

INGREDIENTS

12 Mediterranean king prawns (shrimp)
2 tbsp olive oil
2 tbsp lime juice
2 garlic cloves, crushed
2 fresh green chillies, finely chopped
1 tsp paprika
½ tsp turmeric
1 tbsp finely chopped coriander
salt

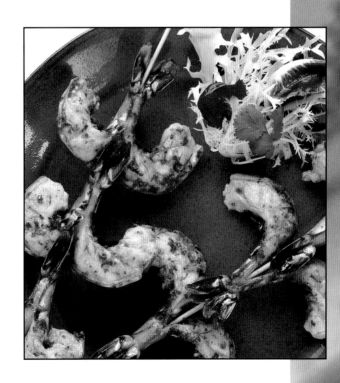

Duck with mango and ginger

Serves 4

METHOD

Mix the soy sauce and sherry in a small bowl. Add the duck and stir well to coat, then leave to marinate for 10 minutes. remove the duck from the marinade and set aside.

Blend the cornflour with the marinade and 3 tbsp water. Cut the mango on either side of the stone, then peel and cut into slices. Heat the oil in a wok or frying pan and stir-fry the duck for 3 minutes, then remove.

Add the spring onions, garlic, ginger and cucumber to the pan and stir-fry for 2 minutes. Return the duck to the pan, stir in the cornflour mixture and cook until thickened. Add the mango slices and heat through. Serve with noodles or boiled rice.

INGREDIENTS

2 tbsp soy sauce
2 tbsp sherry
4 duck breasts, skinned and thinly sliced
2 tsp cornflour
1 mango
2 tbsp groundnut oil
1 bunch spring onions, cut into 4cm/1½inch lengths
2 garlic cloves, chopped
2.5cm/1inch piece fresh root ginger, finely chopped
15cm/6inch piece cucumber, halved and thickly sliced

Sweet and sour chicken

Serves 4

METHOD

In a bowl, mix together the vinegar, honey, soy sauce, tomato ketchup, cornflour and seasoning until smooth. Drain the pineapple and set aside, reserving the syrup; make up to 175ml (6fl oz) with water, then add to the bowl.

Heat the oil in a pan and stir-fry the chicken for 3-4 minutes until golden. Remove from the pan. Add the garlic, peppers and onion to the pan and stir-fry for 4 minutes. Add the cornflour mixture with the chicken and pineapple and cook, stirring, until thickened. Simmer for 3 minutes. Serve with boiled rice.

INGREDIENTS

2 tbsp wine vinegar
1 tbsp clear honey
1 tbsp soy sauce
2 tbsp tomato ketchup
1 tbsp cornflour
salt and pepper to taste
200g/7oz tinned pineapple chunks in syrup
2 tbsp groundnut oil
350g/12oz boneless chicken breast, cut into chunks
2 garlic cloves, chopped
1 red pepper, cored, seeded and cut into 2.5cm/1inch squares
1 green pepper, cored, seeded and cut into 2.5cm/1inch squares
1 onion, chopped

Special fried rice

Serves 2

METHOD

This dish can be served as an accompaniment or a fulfilling snack. Heat 5ml (1 tsp) of the oil in a small frying pan and pour in the egg to make a thin omelette.

The egg will be cooked almost immediately, so remove from the pan, roll up the omelette and slice finely. Set to one side. Heat the remaining oil in a large frying pan or wok then add the garlic and onion and cook for another 3 minutes. Add the remaining ingredients and stir-fry for about 5 minutes, until vegetables are heated through but still a bit crunchy. Serve scattered with the omelette strips.

INGREDIENTS

250g/8oz cooked rice, cooled
15ml/1 tbsp groundnut oil
1 egg, beaten lightly
1 garlic clove, crushed
1 small onion, cut in wedges
300g/10oz of mixed vegetables (e.g. carrot, peppers, beans), cut into bite-sized pieces
200g/6½oz thin sliced ham or chicken, cut into strips
45ml/3 tbsp soy sauce
2 tbsp ketchup or tomato purée

Spiced chicken parcels

Serves 4

METHOD

Put the chicken into a dish. Mix together half of the wine or sherry and the honey then mix with the chicken. Sprinkle with the spices and orange rind and stir together.

Blend the remaining wine with the sesame oil, stir into the bowl with the spring onions. Cover and leave to marinate in the refrigerator overnight.

Return the chicken to room temperature. Cut a 20cm (8inch) square of greaseproof paper for each piece of chicken. Place a sprig of coriander on each piece of chicken and loosely wrap in the greaseproof paper. Seal the edges of the paper securely.

Half fill a deep fat fryer with oil and heat to 180°C/350°F. Lower in parcels and cook for 8-10 minutes. Remove using a slotted spoon.

INGREDIENTS

700g/1½ lb chicken joints, cut into
5cm/2inch pieces
4 tbsp Shao Hsing wine, or medium sherry
2 tsp clear honey
1¼ tsp grated fresh ginger root
½ tsp freshly ground cinnamon
¾ tsp finely crushed coriander seeds
pinch of Chinese five-spice powder
pinch of Szechuan pepper
2 tbsp grated orange rind
1 tbsp sesame oil
2 spring onions thinly sliced
bunch of coriander
vegetable oil, for deep frying
spring onions, sliced diagonally and
coriander leaves, to garnish

Chicken with ginger

Serves 4

METHOD

With the motor running, drop the garlic and ginger into a blender and chop finely. Add the hoisin sauce, soy sauce, sugar and 4 tbsp water. Mix until smooth. With the point of a sharp knife, cut four or five slashes in each drumstick. Place in a shallow heatproof dish. Pour over the ginger mixture, making sure it goes into the slashes. Turn the chicken to coat, then cover and refrigerate for 8 hours, turning the chicken occasionally.

Return the chicken to room temperature 30 minutes before cooking. Preheat the grill. Grill the chicken, turning occasionally, for about 25 minutes until the juices run clear when pierced with the point of a sharp knife.

INGREDIENTS

3-4 garlic cloves
about 85g/3oz fresh ginger root, coarsely chopped
125 ml/4fl oz hoisin sauce
2 tbsp soy sauce
1½-2 tbsp sugar
8 large chicken drumsticks

Gingered pork and pineapple kebabs

Serves 4

METHOD

Cut the pork into 4cm (1½inch) cubes. Mix together the marinade ingredients, pour over the pork and stir well. Leave for 2-4 hours, stirring once or twice. Cut the pineapple into 4cm (1½inch) cubes. Thread the pieces on to the skewers (see page 25) alternately with the pork.

Cook the egg noodles according to the instructions on the packet. Drain and rinse them in cold water. Place the kebabs underneath a hot grill for about 15 minutes, turning them frequently and brushing with the marinade.

Meanwhile heat the oil in a wok or large frying pan. Add the ginger, then the noodles and toss them in the oil for 1 minute. Add the soy sauce and cook for a further 2-3 minutes. Stir in the spring onions, scatter over a little chopped fresh coriander and serve with the kebabs.

INGREDIENTS

900g/2 lb pork tenderloin
425g/15oz tinned pineapple spears in natural juice or half a fresh pineapple

FOR GINGER AND SOY MARINADE

3 tbsp sunflower oil
3 tbsp light soy sauce
1 tbsp dark soy sauce
4 tbsp juice from pineapple
2 tbsp chopped ginger root
1 red chilli, finely chopped
1 garlic clove, finely chopped

FRIED NOODLES

225g/8oz egg noodles
2 tbsp sunflower oil
½ tsp ground ginger
2 tbsp light soy sauce
4 spring onions, finely chopped
fresh coriander, for garnish

Fish cakes

METHOD

These fish cakes make great party food, or a meal. The dipping sauce is a sweet and sour type, but you could use hoisin, chilli or another sauce of your choice.

Combine the fish cake ingredients and season with salt and pepper. Shape into 10 small patties. Bring the vinegar and honey to the boil in a small pan and boil for 5 minutes until reduced by half. Stir in the chilli and sesame seeds.

Heat the oil in a large frying pan and cook the fish cakes for 3 minutes on each side. Serve as a starter with the dipping sauce or with rice and stir-fried vegetables as a more substantial meal, pouring over the dipping sauce.

INGREDIENTS

330g/11oz fish fillet (e.g. salmon, cod, snapper), minced
6 spring onions, finely sliced
150g/5oz mashed potato
85g/3oz baby corn, finely sliced
75g/2½oz green beans, finely sliced
salt and white or Szechuan pepper
30ml/2tbsp vegetable oil

DIPPING SAUCE

150ml/5fl oz rice or white wine vinegar
45ml/3 tbsp clear honey
1 red chilli, sliced
1 tbsp toasted sesame seeds

Monkfish in fragrant coconut milk

Serves 4

METHOD

Preheat the oven to 180°C/350°F/Gas Mark 4. Put the coconut into a bowl. Pour over the water, stir and leave to melt.

Remove the membrane from the fish. Cut out the central bone and divide the fish into four pieces. Mix together the cardamom, ginger, cumin and chilli and rub evenly into the fish. Put half the shallot and 1 garlic clove into an ovenproof dish that is just large enough to hold the fish in a single layer.

Put the fish on top. Tuck the lemon grass between the pieces and sprinkle the remaining shallot and garlic on top. Pour over the coconut. Cover and bake for 30-40 minutes, until the fish flakes when tested with the point of a sharp knife.

INGREDIENTS

25g/1oz creamed coconut, chopped
150 ml/¼ pint boiling water
1 kg/2¼ lb skinned monkfish
½ tsp ground roasted cardamom
2.5cm/1inch fresh root ginger, finely chopped
½ tsp ground roasted cumin
¼-½ tsp ground chilli
1 shallot, finely chopped
2 garlic cloves, chopped
1 stalk lemon grass, crushed
salt and freshly ground black pepper

Serves 4-6

Sweetcorn and chicken soup

INGREDIENTS

1 chicken breast fillet, about 115g/4oz,
skinned and cubed
10ml/2 tsp light soy sauce
15ml/1 tbsp Chinese rice wine
or dry sherry
1 tsp cornflower
60ml/4 tbsp cold water
5ml/1 tsp sesame oil
30ml/2 tbsp groundnut oil
1 litre/1¾ pints chicken stock
425g/15oz tinned creamed sweetcorn
225g/8oz tinned sweetcorn kernels
2 eggs, beaten
salt and ground black pepper
2-3 spring onion stalks, cut into rounds

METHOD

Mince the chicken in a food processor, taking care not to over-process. Transfer the chicken into a mixing bowl and add the soy sauce, rice wine, cornflower, water, sesame oil and seasoning. Allow to stand for about 15 minutes. Heat the groundnut oil in a wok over a medium heat. Add the ginger and stir-fry for a few seconds. Next, add the stock, creamed sweetcorn and sweetcorn kernels and bring to just below boiling point.

Spoon about 90ml (6 tbsp) of the hot liquid into the chicken mixture and stir until it forms a smooth paste. Return to the heat and slowly bring to the boil, stirring continuously. Slowly pour the beaten eggs into the soup, where they should set in thin threads. Sprinkle the spring onions on the soup and serve immediately.

Serves 6-8

Bon-bon chicken with sesame sauce

INGREDIENTS

1 small chicken
1.2 litre/2 pints water
15ml/1 tbsp sesame oil
shredded cucumber, to garnish

FOR THE SAUCE

30ml/2 tbsp light soy sauce
1 tsp sugar
1 tbsp spring onions, finely chopped
5ml/1 tsp red chilli oil
½ tsp ground Szechuan peppercorns
1 tsp white sesame seeds
2 tbsp tahini

METHOD

Clean the chicken well. Bring the water to a fast boil in a wok then add the chicken. Reduce the heat, cover and cook for 40-45 minutes. Remove from the wok and place in a bowl of cold water for at least an hour. Then, shake off any excess water and dry the chicken well. Once dry, brush on a coating of sesame oil. Carve the meat off the legs, wings and breast and pull the meat off the rest of the bones.

On a flat surface, tenderize the meat with a rolling pin, then tear the meat into shreds with your fingers. Place the meat in a dish with the shredded cucumber around the edge. In a bowl, mix together all the sauce ingredients, keeping a few spring onions to garnish. Pour the sauce over the chicken and serve.

Herb and sesame noodles

METHOD

Cook the egg noodles according to the packet instructions. Meanwhile, heat the oil in a wok then add the sesame seeds and fry for about 30 seconds. Stir in the garlic and herbs.

Drain the noodles thoroughly and add to the wok. Heat through, tossing well together to ensure an even coating of the herb oil. Season with salt and pepper and serve at once, garnished with coriander or parsley.

INGREDIENTS

175g/6oz instant egg noodles
2 tbsp sesame oil
2 tbsp sesame seeds
½ garlic clove, crushed
2 tbsp chopped coriander, basil or mint (or a mixture)
salt and pepper to taste
coriander or parsley leaves to garnish

Five-spiced chinese leaf salad

METHOD

This is a delicious warm salad with a sweet and sour taste which is great as a starter or as an accompaniment. Heat the oils in a wok and add the ginger, five-spice powder and water chestnuts and stir-fry for 2 minutes. Next add the sherry, soy sauce and sugar to the wok and stir.

Add the Chinese leaf to the pan and continue to cook for about 2 minutes, until the leaves are slightly wilted but the white stalks are still crisp. Season with salt and pepper to taste and serve at once, garnished with coriander leaves.

INGREDIENTS

2 tbsp groundnut oil
1 tsp sesame oil
2.5cm/1inch piece fresh root ginger, grated
large pinch of five-spice powder
215g/7oz tinned water chestnuts, drained and sliced
2 tbsp sherry or rice wine
1 tbsp soy sauce
½ tsp soft light brown sugar
1 head Chinese leaf, roughly torn
salt and pepper to taste
coriander leaves to garnish

Chinese noodles and vegetable salad

Serves 6

METHOD

Put the noodles in a large pan of boiling salted water, remove the pan from the heat and leave to stand for 5 minutes. Drain the noodles, rinse them under cold water and drain them again.

Cut the broccoli into very small florets and cut the mangetout in half lengthways. Blanch both in boiling water for about 1 minute then drain and mix with the noodles in a bowl.

Put the ingredients for the dressing in a food processor or blender and mix until smooth. Pour over the salad and toss together. Serve sprinkled with sesame seeds.

INGREDIENTS

175g/6oz egg noodles
175g/6oz broccoli florets
115g/4oz mangetout, trimmed
lightly toasted sesame seeds or black sesame seeds, for garnish

FOR THE DRESSING

2 tbsp white wine vinegar
2 tbsp light soy sauce
1 garlic clove, crushed
2 tsp caster sugar
½ tsp dried hot pepper flakes
½ tsp anchovy paste

Teriyaki turkey

Serves 4

METHOD

Mix the marinade ingredients together in a shallow dish. Add the turkey strips, turn to coat and leave to marinate for about 30 minutes.

To make the fried rice, heat the oil in a frying pan and stir-fry the spring onions for 2 minutes. Add the cumin and fry, stirring, for 1 minute. Add the rice and turn to coat with the spiced oil. Heat through gently, stirring. Cover and keep warm.

Preheat the grill to high. Thread the turkey on to bamboo satay sticks and resemble snakes, using about 3 strips to each stick. Grill for about 2 minutes on each side. Serve with the fried rice, and accompanied by a salad.

INGREDIENTS

500g/1lb turkey strips

FOR THE MARINADE

3 tbsp soy sauce
2 tbsp sherry
2 garlic cloves, crushed
2.5cm/1inch piece fresh root ginger, finely chopped
1 tbsp sesame oil

FRIED RICE

2 tbsp sunflower oil
6 spring onions, chopped
2 tsp ground cumin
500g/1lb cooked rice

Hot green chicken strips

Serves 4

METHOD

In a blender, mix the chillies, garlic, coriander, mint, spring onions lime rind, lime juice, sugar, bitters and 3 tbsp of water to form a runny paste. Arrange the chicken in a single layer, pour over the chilli mixture, cover and leave at room temperature for 2-4 hours.

Remove the chicken from the dish, scraping off the chilli mixture and keeping to one side. With a sharp knife cut the chicken diagonally into thin strips.

Heat the oil in a large frying pan, add the chicken and nuts and stir-fry until the chicken turns white. Add the stock and chilli mixture and simmer for 3 minutes. Mix the cornflour with the soy sauce to form a paste, then stir into the pan. Cook, stirring, until the mixture thickens. Serve with boiled rice.

INGREDIENTS

2 fresh green chillies
2 garlic cloves
3 coriander sprigs
5 mint sprigs
3 plump spring onions
finely grated rind and juice of 1 lime
1 tsp caster sugar
1 tsp angostura bitters
350g/12oz skinned and boned
chicken breasts
3 tbsp peanut oil
2 tbsp cashew nuts
200ml/7 fl oz chicken stock
2 tsp cornflour
2 tbsp soy sauce
boiled rice, to serve

Coconut rice

Serves 6

METHOD

Heat the oil in a large saucepan, add the onion and cook until it is golden. Stir in the rice, cinnamon stick, water, salt and creamed coconut. Simmer for about 15-20 minutes until the rice is just tender and the liquid is absorbed.

While the rice is cooking, melt the butter in a wok or frying pan, then add the desiccated coconut and stir-fry until it is just golden. Stir the desiccated coconut and the coriander into the cooked rice and season with salt and pepper if necessary.

INGREDIENTS

2 tbsp sunflower oil
1 small onion, finely chopped
225g/8oz long-grain rice
1 cinnamon stick
600ml/1 pint water
½ tsp salt
55g/2oz creamed coconut cut into small pieces
30g/1oz butter
30g/1oz desiccated coconut
2 tbsp chopped fresh coriander or parsley
salt and freshly ground black pepper

Thai prawn and mint salad

Serves 4

INGREDIENTS

**32 uncooked, unshelled prawns (shrimp),
about 900g/2lb
1½-2 stalks lemon grass, finely chopped
4 tbsp fish sauce
4 tbsp lime juice
1 tbsp finely chopped garlic
3 fresh red chillies, finely chopped
25g/1oz spring onions, white
part only, sliced
about 55g/2oz small mint leaves
lettuce leaves, tomato wedges and small
mint sprigs, to serve**

METHOD

Bring a wok of water to the boil, add the prawns and bring to simmering point. Drain and leave the prawns until cool enough to handle, then remove the shells, legs and heads. Run the points of a sharp knife along the back of each prawn and remove the dark thread. Leave to cool, but do not chill.

Mix together the lemon grass, fish sauce, lime juice, garlic, chillies, spring onions, and mint leaves, crushing lightly with the back of a spoon. Toss in the prawns. Taste and add more mint and lemon grass if necessary.

Arrange a few lettuce leaves on a large serving plate or in a bowl, pile the prawn mixture on top and add tomato wedges and mint sprigs. Serve immediately.

Chicken chow mein

Serves 4

METHOD

Cook the noodles in boiling salted water according to packet instructions. Drain well and toss in the sesame oil. Beat the eggs with seasoning in a bowl. Heat 1 tsp oil in a wok or frying pan then pour in half of the egg mixture to make a large thin omelette and cook on both sides.

When cooked, turn out and cut into strips. Repeat with the rest of the egg mixture. Heat the remaining oil in a wok and stir-fry the chicken for 2 minutes; remove. Add the garlic, ginger, red pepper, mushrooms and spring onions and stir-fry for 2 minutes.

Add the noodles, sherry, soy sauce and chicken and cook, stirring, for 2 minutes. Stir in the egg strips and cashew nuts and heat through. Serve immediately.

INGREDIENTS

175g/6oz Chinese egg noodles
2 tsp sesame oil
2 eggs
salt and pepper to taste
2 tbsp groundnut oil
350g/12oz chicken breast strips
1 garlic clove, chopped
2.5cm/1inch fresh root ginger, chopped
1 red pepper, cored, seeded and thinly sliced
125g/4oz shiitake or chestnut mushrooms, sliced
6-8 spring onions, cut into 3.5cm/1½inch lengths
2 tbsp sherry
2 tbsp soy sauce
50g/2oz roasted cashew nuts

Serves 4-6

Thai green curry with prawns

INGREDIENTS

30ml/2 tbsp vegetable oil
2 tbsp green curry paste
450g/1lb King prawns, shelled
and deveined
4 kaffir lime leaves, torn
1 stalk lemon grass, finely chopped
250ml/8fl oz coconut milk
30ml/2 tbsp fish sauce
½ cucumber, seeded and cut into
thin batons
10-15 basil leaves
4 green chillies, sliced, to garnish

METHOD

Heat the oil in a frying pan then add the curry paste and fry until bubbling. Next add the King prawns, kaffir lime leaves and lemon grass and continue to cook until the prawns are pink, which should take between 1 and 2 minutes.

Slowly stir in the coconut milk and bring to a gentle boil, taking care not to heat too rapidly as this will scorch the sauce. Simmer over a low heat, stirring occasionally, for between 5-7 minutes or until the prawns are thoroughly cooked. Finally, add the fish sauce, cucumber, and basil. Place on a bed of rice and top with the green chillies to garnish.

Serves 6-8

Vietnamese Spring Rolls

INGREDIENTS

6 dried Chinese mushrooms, soaked in
hot water for 30 minutes
225g/8oz lean ground pork
225g/4oz uncooked prawns, peeled,
deveined and chopped
115g/4oz white crabmeat
1 carrot, shredded
50g/2oz cellophane noodles, soaked in
water, drained and cut into short lengths
4 spring onions, finely chopped
30ml/2 tbsp fish sauce
juice of 1 lime
freshly ground black pepper
24 x 10cm/4inch Vietnamese rice sheets
oil for deep frying
lettuce leaves, cucumber slices, and
coriander leaves to garnish

METHOD

Drain the mushrooms.and thinly slice the caps into a bowl. Add the pork, prawns, crabmeat, carrot, cellophane noodles, spring onions and garlic. Season with the fish sauce, lime juice and pepper. Set the mixture aside for about 30 minutes to allow the flavours to blend.

Place a rice sheet on a flat surface and brush with warm water until it is pliable. Place about 10ml (2 tsp) of the filling near the edge of the rice sheet. Fold the sides over the filling, fold in the two ends, then roll up, sealing the ends of the roll with a little water. Heat the oil for frying to 180°C/350°F. Add the rolls, a few at a time, and fry until golden brown and crisp. Drain on kitchen paper.

Serves 4-6

Noodles with aubergine

METHOD

Cut the aubergine into strips and place in a colander or sieve. Rinse with cold water, then sprinkle with the salt. Leave to stand for 20 minutes then rinse thoroughly and drain well. Cook the egg noodles according to the packet instructions. Meanwhile, heat the groundnut oil in a wok. Add the aubergine, garlic, red pepper and bamboo shoots and stir-fry for 2-3 minutes until the aubergine is soft.

Add the yellow bean sauce and heat through. Season with Szechuan pepper to taste.

Drain the noodles and toss in the sesame oil. Transfer to a warmed serving dish and top with the aubergine mixture to serve.

INGREDIENTS

250g/8oz aubergine
1½ tsp salt
250/8oz thread egg noodles
3-4 tbsp groundnut oil
1 garlic clove, crushed
½ red pepper, seeded and cut into strips
227g/8oz tinned bamboo shoots, drained
3 tbsp yellow bean sauce
¼-½ tsp Szechuan peppercorns, crushed
1-2 tsp sesame oil

Serves 4

Indonesian-style satay chicken

METHOD

Take 8 wooden skewers (see page 25). Heat the oil in the wok then add the onion, ginger and garlic. Cook for about 2-3 minutes until softened but not browned. Remove with a slotted spoon and drain on kitchen paper. Next, add the chicken pieces to the wok and stir-fry for 3-4 minutes until golden on all sides. When cooked, thread onto the skewers and keep warm.

Add the creamed coconut to the hot wok in small pieces and stir-fry until melted. Add the chilli sauce, peanut butter and ginger mixture and simmer for 2 minutes. Stir in the sugar, milk and salt, and simmer for a further 3 minutes. Serve the skewered chicken hot, with a dish of the hot dipping sauce sprinkled with the roasted peanuts.

INGREDIENTS

50g/2oz raw peanuts
45ml/3 tbsp vegetable oil
1 small onion, finely chopped
2.5cm/1inch fresh root ginger, peeled and finely chopped
1 garlic clove, crushed
675g/1½lb chicken thighs, skinned and cut into cubes
90g/3½oz creamed coconut, roughly chopped
1 tbsp chilli sauce
4 tbsp crunchy peanut butter
1 tsp soft dark brown sugar
150ml/¼ pint milk
¼ tsp salt

Index